CW01208705

The Latest Tower Vortx Dual Basket Air Fryer Oven Cookbook

1600 Days Crispy and Healthy Air Frying Recipes, Perfect Homemade Meals for Everyone

Juliana J. Cook

CONTENTS

INTRODUCTION....4

WHAT EXACTLY IS AIR FRYING?.4

Can I Skip the Oil When I Use My Tower Vortx Dual Basket Air Fryer Oven? 5
Tips for Using a Tower Vortx Dual Basket Air Fryer Oven....6

MEASUREMENT CONVERSIONS 7

BREAKFAST & SNACKS AND FRIES RECIPES....9

Baba Ganoush....10
Bocconcini Balls....10
Toad In The Hole, Breakfast Style....11
Halloumi Fries....11
Potato & Chorizo Frittata....12
Healthy Stuffed Peppers....12
Breakfast Eggs & Spinach....13
European Pancakes....13
Breakfast "pop Tarts"....14
Easy Cheese & Bacon Toasties....14
Raspberry Breakfast Pockets....15
Pitta Pizza....15
Your Favourite Breakfast Bacon....15
Blueberry Bread....16
Breakfast Doughnuts....16
Blanket Breakfast Eggs....16
Monte Cristo Breakfast Sandwich....17
Sweet Potato Fries....17
French Toast Slices....18
Mexican Breakfast Burritos....18

SAUCES & SNACK AND APPETISER RECIPES.... 19

Spicy Egg Rolls....20
Beetroot Crisps....20
Waffle Fries....21
Air-fried Pickles....21
Tasty Pumpkin Seeds....21
Focaccia Bread....22
Scotch Eggs....22
Mini Calzones....23
Snack Style Falafel....23
Bacon Smokies....24
Pretzel Bites....24
Pasta Chips....25
Thai Bites....25
Jalapeño Poppers....25
Pepperoni Bread....26
Peppers With Aioli Dip....26
Corn Nuts....27
Sweet Potato Crisps....27
Salt And Vinegar Chips....28
Onion Pakoda....28

POULTRY RECIPES.... 29

Healthy Bang Bang Chicken....30
Chicken Tikka....30
Chicken Jalfrezi....31
Crunchy Chicken Tenders....31
Chicken Tikka Masala....32
Thai Turkey Burgers....32
Orange Chicken....33
Keto Tandoori Chicken....33
Nashville Chicken....34

Chicken Balls, Greek-style 34
Chicken Fajitas....................................35
Honey Cajun Chicken Thighs 35
Hawaiian Chicken....................................36
Air Fryer Chicken Thigh Schnitzel....................................36
Air Fried Maple Chicken Thighs 37
Buffalo Chicken Wontons 37
Pizza Chicken Nuggets 38
Chicken Fried Rice 38
Turkey Cutlets In Mushroom Sauce 39
Chicken And Wheat Stir Fry....................................39

BEEF & LAMB AND PORK RECIPES 40

Steak Popcorn Bites 41
Hamburgers....................................41
Char Siu Buffalo 42
Buttermilk Pork Chops 42
Steak Dinner....................................43
Beef Bulgogi Burgers....................................43
Salt And Pepper Belly Pork 44
Tender Ham Steaks 44
Mustard Pork Tenderloin 44
Beef Wellington 45
Steak Fajitas....................................45
Sausage Gnocchi One Pot....................................46
Asparagus & Steak Parcels....................................46
Jamaican Jerk Pork 47
Pork Belly With Crackling....................................47
Beef Kebobs....................................47
Traditional Pork Chops 48
Meatloaf....................................48
Meatballs In Tomato Sauce....................................49
Pork Chops With Honey 49

FISH & SEAFOOD RECIPES.......... 50

Lemon Pepper Shrimp 51
Air Fryer Mussels 51
Crispy Nacho Prawns....................................52
Salmon Patties....................................52
Air Fried Scallops 52
Store-cupboard Fishcakes 53
Tandoori Salmon....................................53
Crunchy Fish....................................54
Garlic Butter Salmon 54
Shrimp With Yum Yum Sauce....................................55
Coconut Shrimp 55
Honey Sriracha Salmon 56
Copycat Fish Fingers 56
Beer Battered Fish Tacos 57
Mahi Fish Tacos....................................57
Shrimp Wrapped With Bacon 58
Peppery Lemon Shrimp 58
Furikake Salmon 58
Lobster Tails....................................59
Cod In Parma Ham....................................59

VEGETARIAN & VEGAN RECIPES60

Saganaki....................................61
Bbq Soy Curls....................................61
Spinach And Feta Croissants 62
Stuffed Peppers 62
Lentil Burgers 63
Falafel Burgers....................................63
Camembert & Soldiers....................................64
Roasted Vegetable Pasta....................................64
Roasted Cauliflower....................................64
Spicy Spanish Potatoes 65
Buffalo Cauliflower Bites 65
Rainbow Vegetables....................................66
Mushroom Pasta....................................66
Roast Vegetables 67
Roast Cauliflower & Broccoli....................................67
Ravioli Air Fryer Style....................................67
Artichoke Pasta 68
Veggie Lasagne 68
Air Fryer Cheese Sandwich 69
Broccoli Cheese 69

SIDE DISHES RECIPES 70

Air Fryer Eggy Bread... 71
Carrot & Parmesan Chips 71
Bbq Beetroot Crisps.. 72
Honey Roasted Parsnips 72
Tex Mex Hash Browns.. 72
Onion Rings 73
Stuffing Filled Pumpkin 73
Orange Sesame Cauliflower.................................... 74
Stuffed Jacket Potatoes 74
Spicy Green Beans.. 75
Cauliflower With Hot Sauce And Blue Cheese Sauce 75
Yorkshire Puddings 76
Alternative Stuffed Potatoes 76
Corn On The Cob.. 77
Ricotta Stuffed Aubergine...................................... 77
Ranch-style Potatoes.. 78
Roasted Okra.. 78
Super Easy Fries 78
Potato Wedges.. 79
Mediterranean Vegetables...................................... 79

DESSERTS RECIPES 80

Oat-covered Banana Fritters 81
Peach Pies 81
Pecan & Molasses Flapjack 82
Chocolate Mug Cake... 82
Sweet Potato Dessert Fries...................................... 82
Lemon Pies.. 83
White Chocolate Pudding 83
Grain-free Millionaire's Shortbread......................... 84
Melting Moments.. 84
Cinnamon Biscuit Bites 85
Chocolate Orange Fondant 85
Apple Fritters 86
Apple And Cinnamon Puff Pastry Pies 86
Birthday Cheesecake... 87
Mini Egg Buns 87
Butter Cake 88
Zebra Cake 88
Brazilian Pineapple 89
Apple Pie.. 89
Chocolate Eclairs 90

APPENDIX : RECIPES INDEX 91

INTRODUCTION

Hi, I'm Juliana J. Cook. Always loved food and cooking. Some of my earliest memories are perusing recipes and then making pudding with my dad on Sundays.

I have an amazing husband, three beautiful children, and two playful and lively puppies. I'm so lucky to live in a great village and have a job that I really enjoy.

On Christmas 2015 I moved to the Midlands to train as a Pediatric Nurse where I met and married my husband Dan. When we had our oldest, I was working and caring for him and couldn't be with him when I was busy, I realized that being perpetually sleep deprived and neglecting a child's development was not what I wanted in life and I left Nursing position.

I've been a full time mom and wife since early 2017, and now I do have time and lots of hobbies, so I started reading cookbooks and stocking up on ingredients and haven't stopped cooking since! I am blessed to spend a lot of time cooking, baking, creating and trying new foods and recipes, and my son and husband love them!

There is also real satisfaction in cooking from scratch, especially creating and adapting recipes - I love it. However, like most of us, I often have to get meals to the table very quickly. So if you like inspiring recipes and exciting meals that don't take an entire day to whip up, this latest Tower Vortx Double Basket Air Fryer Oven Cookbook is for you. A lot of what I make is seasonal and almost everything is quick and easy. Here you'll find recipes for everything from drinks and breakfasts to main dishes, side dishes and special occasions.

Now, let's go to the kitchen and have fun!

What Exactly Is Air Frying?

Looking for a healthier alternative to deep-frying? Meet the air fryer, your new favorite gadget. Check out these air-fryer recipes for crispy chicken wings, fried pickles, coconut shrimp—and desserts, too!

For starters, the air fryer allows us to make crispy foods that taste similar to the deep-fried version but without all of the extra oil. Definitely sounds like a win, but is it really healthy?

An air fryer is basically a hybrid between a deep fryer and a convection oven. The air fryer contains a fry basket that allows food to be suspended and accessible to heat from all sides—great for making things nice and crispy.

However, instead of being placed in hot oil, the food is exposed to very hot, circulating air—similar to the convection oven. If you prefer to eat fried food, then the air fryer is definitely a good choice. Still, the air fryer isn't a magic machine for making any food definitively "healthy."

So, now that we know how the air fryer works, how does it compare to traditional cooking methods?

Enter the Air Fryer - the appliance that guarantees the taste, texture, and golden brownness of deep-fried foods, without more fat and calories. When comparing the air fryer to the oven, the two appliances are similar in functionality, except the former allows you to cook food in a shorter period of time.

The air fryer isn't a "free pass" to eat unlimited amounts of higher-calorie foods just because it's better than deep frying. It's also important to remember that the main benefit of air frying over deep frying is the lack of oil, so if you begin adding significant amounts of oil to air-fried foods, the benefits may not be quite as drastic.

Eating too much fried food can easily lead to overeating. That said, air frying significantly reduces the amount of oil absorbed by food compared to deep frying. This is a benefit of using an air fryer, as less oil generally results in fewer calories consumed, which can reduce the risk of weight gain, obesity, and more.

Instead, the real driver of "what is healthy" is the kind of foods you eat and put in the air fryer. Nutrient-dense foods like fruits, veggies, whole grains, fatty fish and lean meats are generally just as nutritious in the air fryer as in the oven.

Can I Skip the Oil When I Use My Tower Vortx Dual Basket Air Fryer Oven?

Most air fryer manufacturers and recipes recommend that you either toss or spray foods with at least a little oil. However, I've found it's not necessary. Food comes out just as crispy without a thin coating of oil. Of course, a little bit of oil helps with the crisping.

From baked potatoes to ultra-crispy bacon, these are staple recipes you'll come back to again and again. And they're a perfect starting point if you're just getting started with air frying.

Tips for Using a Tower Vortx Dual Basket Air Fryer Oven

An air fryer can be a great addition to your kitchen beyond being a healthier alternative to a deep fryer: It can also save time spent cooking and cleaning. However, here are some health-focused tips to keep in mind when using an air fryer:

Read the instructions: Most air fryers require you to leave at least five inches of space above the exhaust vent. Otherwise, they become a fire hazard.

Use minimal amounts of oil: Toss or brush food with about one to two teaspoons of oil per serving. Not only can too much oil up the calorie and fat content, but it can also cause smoking, making food taste bad and impacting your health by producing free radicals that can harm cells.

Avoid aerosol sprays: Aerosol cooking oils can potentially break down the air fryer's non-stick basket, releasing toxic fumes.

Pair with other cooking methods: While air fryers are great, switch up your cooking methods throughout the week via sautéing, slow cooking, and steaming. This will further reduce your exposure to chemicals like acrylamide. It also ensures you enjoy a wider variety of foods—not just those compatible with air fryers—which increases the spectrum of nutrients you consume.

Measurement Conversions

BASIC KITCHEN CONVERSIONS & EQUIVALENTS

DRY MEASUREMENTS CONVERSION CHART

3 TEASPOONS = 1 TABLESPOON = 1/16 CUP

6 TEASPOONS = 2 TABLESPOONS = 1/8 CUP

12 TEASPOONS = 4 TABLESPOONS = 1/4 CUP

24 TEASPOONS = 8 TABLESPOONS = 1/2 CUP

36 TEASPOONS = 12 TABLESPOONS = 3/4 CUP

48 TEASPOONS = 16 TABLESPOONS = 1 CUP

METRIC TO US COOKING CONVERSIONS

OVEN TEMPERATURES

120 °C = 250 °F

160 °C = 320 °F

180° C = 350 °F

205 °C = 400 °F

220 °C = 425 °F

LIQUID MEASUREMENTS CONVERSION CHART

8 FLUID OUNCES = 1 CUP = 1/2 PINT = 1/4 QUART

16 FLUID OUNCES = 2 CUPS = 1 PINT = 1/2 QUART

32 FLUID OUNCES = 4 CUPS = 2 PINTS = 1 QUART = 1/4 GALLON

128 FLUID OUNCES = 16 CUPS = 8 PINTS = 4 QUARTS = 1 GALLON

BAKING IN GRAMS

1 CUP FLOUR = 140 GRAMS

1 CUP SUGAR = 150 GRAMS

1 CUP POWDERED SUGAR = 160 GRAMS

1 CUP HEAVY CREAM = 235 GRAMS

VOLUME

1 MILLILITER = 1/5 TEASPOON

5 ML = 1 TEASPOON

15 ML = 1 TABLESPOON

240 ML = 1 CUP OR 8 FLUID OUNCES

1 LITER = 34 FL. OUNCES

WEIGHT

1 GRAM = .035 OUNCES

100 GRAMS = 3.5 OUNCES

500 GRAMS = 1.1 POUNDS

1 KILOGRAM = 35 OUNCES

US TO METRIC COOKING CONVERSIONS

1/5 TSP = 1 ML

1 TSP = 5 ML

1 TBSP = 15 ML

1 FL OUNCE = 30 ML

1 CUP = 237 ML

1 PINT (2 CUPS) = 473 ML

1 QUART (4 CUPS) = .95 LITER

1 GALLON (16 CUPS) = 3.8 LITERS

1 OZ = 28 GRAMS

1 POUND = 454 GRAMS

BUTTER

1 CUP BUTTER = 2 STICKS = 8 OUNCES = 230 GRAMS = 8 TABLESPOONS

WHAT DOES 1 CUP EQUAL

1 CUP = 8 FLUID OUNCES

1 CUP = 16 TABLESPOONS

1 CUP = 48 TEASPOONS

1 CUP = 1/2 PINT

1 CUP = 1/4 QUART

1 CUP = 1/16 GALLON

1 CUP = 240 ML

BAKING PAN CONVERSIONS

1 CUP ALL-PURPOSE FLOUR = 4.5 OZ

1 CUP ROLLED OATS = 3 OZ 1 LARGE EGG = 1.7 OZ

1 CUP BUTTER = 8 OZ 1 CUP MILK = 8 OZ

1 CUP HEAVY CREAM = 8.4 OZ

1 CUP GRANULATED SUGAR = 7.1 OZ

1 CUP PACKED BROWN SUGAR = 7.75 OZ

1 CUP VEGETABLE OIL = 7.7 OZ

1 CUP UNSIFTED POWDERED SUGAR = 4.4 OZ

BAKING PAN CONVERSIONS

9-INCH ROUND CAKE PAN = 12 CUPS

10-INCH TUBE PAN =16 CUPS

11-INCH BUNDT PAN = 12 CUPS

9-INCH SPRINGFORM PAN = 10 CUPS

9 X 5 INCH LOAF PAN = 8 CUPS

9-INCH SQUARE PAN = 8 CUPS

Breakfast & Snacks And Fries Recipes

Baba Ganoush

Servings: 4 | Cooking Time:xx

Ingredients:

- 1 large aubergine/eggplant, sliced in half lengthways
- ½ teaspoon salt
- 5 tablespoons olive oil
- 1 bulb garlic
- 30 g/2 tablespoons tahini or nut butter
- 2 tablespoons freshly squeezed lemon juice
- ½ teaspoon ground cumin
- ¼ teaspoon smoked paprika
- salt and freshly ground black pepper
- 3 tablespoons freshly chopped flat-leaf parsley

Directions:

1. Preheat the air-fryer to 200°C/400°F.
2. Lay the aubergine/eggplant halves cut side up. Sprinkle over the salt, then drizzle over 1 tablespoon of oil. Cut the top off the garlic bulb, brush the exposed cloves with a little olive oil, then wrap in foil. Place the aubergine/eggplant and foil-wrapped garlic in the preheated air-fryer and air-fry for 15–20 minutes until the inside of the aubergine is soft and buttery in texture.
3. Scoop the flesh of the aubergine into a bowl. Squeeze out about 1 tablespoon of the cooked garlic and add to the bowl with the remaining 4 tablespoons of olive oil, the tahini/nut butter, lemon juice, spices and salt and pepper to taste. Mix well and serve with fresh flat-leaf parsley sprinkled over.

Bocconcini Balls

Servings: 2 | Cooking Time:xx

Ingredients:

- 70 g/½ cup plus ½ tablespoon plain/all-purpose flour (gluten-free if you wish)
- 1 egg, beaten
- 70 g/1 cup dried breadcrumbs (gluten-free if you wish; see page 9)
- 10 bocconcini

Directions:

1. Preheat the air-fryer to 200°C/400°F.
2. Place the flour, egg and breadcrumbs on 3 separate plates. Dip each bocconcini ball first in the flour to coat, then the egg, shaking off any excess before rolling in the breadcrumbs.
3. Add the breaded bocconcini to the preheated air-fryer and air-fry for 5 minutes (no need to turn them during cooking). Serve immediately.

Toad In The Hole, Breakfast Style

Servings: 4 | Cooking Time:xx

Ingredients:

- 1 sheet of puff pastry (defrosted)
- 4 eggs
- 4 tbsp grated cheese (cheddar works well)
- 4 slices of cooked ham, cut into pieces
- Chopped fresh herbs of your choice

Directions:

1. Preheat your air fryer to 200ºC
2. Take your pastry sheet and place it on a flat surface, cutting it into four pieces
3. Take two of the pastry sheets and place them inside your fryer, cooking for up to 8 minutes, until done
4. Remove the pastry and flatten the centre down with a spoon, to form a deep hole
5. Add a tablespoon of the cheese and a tablespoon of the ham into the hole
6. Crack one egg into the hole
7. Return the pastry to the air fryer and cook for another 6 minutes, or until the egg is done as you like it
8. Remove and allow to cool
9. Repeat the process with the rest of the pastry remaining
10. Sprinkle fresh herbs on top and serve

Halloumi Fries

Servings: 2 | Cooking Time:xx

Ingredients:

- 225 g/8 oz. halloumi
- 40 g/heaped ¼ cup plain/all-purpose flour (gluten-free if you wish)
- ½ teaspoon sweet smoked paprika
- ½ teaspoon dried oregano
- ¼ teaspoon mild chilli/chili powder
- olive oil or avocado oil, for spraying

Directions:

1. Preheat the air-fryer to 180ºC/350ºF.
2. Slice the halloumi into fries roughly 2 x 1.5 cm/¾ x ⅝ in.
3. Mix the flour and seasoning in a bowl and dip each halloumi stick into the flour to coat. Spray with a little oil.
4. Add the fries to the preheated air-fryer and air-fry for 5 minutes. Serve immediately.

Potato & Chorizo Frittata

Servings: 2 | Cooking Time:xx

Ingredients:

- 3 eggs
- 1 sliced chorizo sausage
- 1 potato, boiled and cubed
- 50g feta cheese
- 50g frozen sweetcorn
- A pinch of salt
- 1 tbsp olive oil

Directions:

1. Add a little olive oil to the frying basket
2. Add the corn, potato, and sliced chorizo to the basket
3. Cook at 180ºC until the sausage is a little brown
4. In a small bowl, beat together the eggs with a little seasoning
5. Pour the eggs into the pan
6. Crumble the feta on top
7. Cook for 5 minutes
8. Remove and serve in slices

Healthy Stuffed Peppers

Servings: 2 | Cooking Time:xx

Ingredients:

- 1 large bell pepper, deseeded and cut into halves
- 1 tsp olive oil
- 4 large eggs
- Salt and pepper to taste

Directions:

1. Take your peppers and rub a little olive oil on the edges
2. Into each pepper, crack one egg and season with salt and pepper
3. You will need to insert a trivet into your air fryer to hold the peppers, and then arrange the peppers evenly
4. Set your fryer to 200ºC and cook for 13 minutes
5. Once cooked, remove and serve with a little more seasoning, if required

Breakfast Eggs & Spinach

Servings: 4 | Cooking Time:xx

Ingredients:
- 500g wilted, fresh spinach
- 200g sliced deli ham
- 1 tbsp olive oil
- 4 eggs
- 4 tsp milk
- Salt and pepper to taste
- 1 tbsp butter for cooking

Directions:
1. Preheat your air fryer to 180°C
2. You will need 4 small ramekin dishes, coated with a little butter
3. Arrange the wilted spinach, ham, 1 teaspoon of milk and 1 egg into each ramekin and season with a little salt and pepper
4. Place in the fryer 15 to 20 minutes, until the egg is cooked to your liking
5. Allow to cool before serving

European Pancakes

Servings: 5 | Cooking Time:xx

Ingredients:
- 3 large eggs
- 130g flour
- 140ml whole milk
- 2 tbsp unsweetened apple sauce
- A pinch of salt

Directions:
1. Set your fryer to 200°C and add five ramekins inside to heat up
2. Place all your ingredients inside a blender to combine
3. Spray the ramekins with a little cooking spray
4. Pour the batter into the ramekins carefully
5. Fry for between 6-8 minutes, depending on your preference
6. Serve with your favourite toppings

Breakfast “pop Tarts”

Servings: 6 | Cooking Time:xx

Ingredients:

- 2 slices of prepared pie crust, shortbread or filo will work fine
- 2 tbsp strawberry jam
- 60ml plain yogurt
- 1 tsp cornstarch
- 1 tsp Stevia sweetener
- 2 tbsp cream cheese
- A drizzle of olive oil

Directions:

1. Lay your pie crust flat and cut into 6 separate rectangular pieces
2. In a small bowl, mix together the cornstarch and the jam
3. Spread 1 tablespoon of the mixture on top of the crust
4. Fold each crust over to form the tart
5. Seal down the edges using a fork
6. Arrange your tarts inside the frying basket and spray with a little olive oil
7. Heat to 175°C and cook for 10 minutes
8. Meanwhile, combine the yogurt, cream cheese and Stevia in a bowl
9. Remove the tarts and allow to cool
10. Once cool, add the frosting on top and sprinkle with the sugar sprinkles

Easy Cheese & Bacon Toasties

Servings: 2 | Cooking Time:xx

Ingredients:

- 4 slices of sandwich bread
- 2 slices of cheddar cheese
- 5 slices of pre-cooked bacon
- 1 tbsp melted butter
- 2 slices of mozzarella cheese

Directions:

1. Take the bread and spread the butter onto one side of each slice
2. Place one slice of bread into the fryer basket, buttered side facing downwards
3. Place the cheddar on top, followed by the bacon, mozzarella and the other slice of bread on top, buttered side upwards
4. Set your fryer to 170°C
5. Cook for 4 minutes and then turn over and cook for another 3 minutes
6. Serve whilst still hot

Raspberry Breakfast Pockets

Servings: 1 | Cooking Time:xx

Ingredients:

- 2 slices of sandwich bread
- 1 tbsp soft cream cheese
- 1 tbsp raspberry jam
- 1 tbsp milk
- 1 egg

Directions:

1. Take one slice of the bread and add one tablespoon of jam into the middle
2. Take the second slice and add the cream cheese into the middle
3. Using a blunt knife, spread the jam and the cheese across the bread, but don't go to the outer edges
4. Take a small bowl and whisk the eggs and the milk together
5. Set your fryer to 190ºC and spray with a little oil
6. Dip your sandwich into the egg and arrange inside your fryer
7. Cook for 5 minutes on the first side, turn and cook for another 2 minutes

Pitta Pizza

Servings: 2 | Cooking Time:xx

Ingredients:

- 2 round wholemeal pitta breads
- 3 tablespoons passata/strained tomatoes
- 4 tablespoons grated mozzarella
- 1 teaspoon dried oregano
- 1 teaspoon olive oil
- basil leaves, to serve

Directions:

1. Preheat the air-fryer to 200ºC/400ºF.
2. Pop the pittas into the preheated air-fryer and air-fry for 1 minute.
3. Remove the pittas from the air-fryer and spread a layer of the passata/strained tomatoes on the pittas, then scatter over the mozzarella, oregano and oil. Return to the air-fryer and air-fry for a further 4 minutes. Scatter over the basil leaves and serve immediately.

Your Favourite Breakfast Bacon

Servings: 2 | Cooking Time:xx

Ingredients:

- 4-5 rashers of lean bacon, fat cut off
- Salt and pepper for seasoning

Directions:

1. Line your air fryer basket with parchment paper
2. Place the bacon in the basket
3. Set the fryer to 200ºC
4. Cook for 10 minutes for crispy. If you want it very crispy, cook for another 2 minutes

Blueberry Bread

Servings: 8 | Cooking Time:xx

Ingredients:

- 260ml milk
- 3 eggs
- 25g protein powder
- 400g frozen blueberries
- 600g bisquick or pancake mixture

Directions:

1. Take a large mixing bowl and combine all ingredients until smooth
2. Preheat the air fryer to 250ºC
3. Place the mixture into a loaf tin
4. Place the tin into the air fryer and cook for 30 minutes
5. A toothpick should come out clean if the bread is cooked

Breakfast Doughnuts

Servings: 4 | Cooking Time:xx

Ingredients:

- 1 packet of Pillsbury Grands
- 5 tbsp raspberry jam
- 1 tbsp melted butter
- 5 tbsp sugar

Directions:

1. Preheat your air fryer to 250ºC
2. Place the Pillsbury Grands into the air fryer and cook for around 5m minutes
3. Remove and place to one side
4. Take a large bowl and add the sugar
5. Coat the doughnuts in the melted butter, coating evenly
6. Dip into the sugar and coat evenly once more
7. Using an icing bag, add the jam into the bag and pipe an even amount into each doughnut
8. Eat warm or cold

Blanket Breakfast Eggs

Servings: 2 | Cooking Time:xx

Ingredients:

- 2 eggs
- 2 slices of sandwich bread
- Olive oil spray
- Salt and pepper to taste

Directions:

1. Preheat your air fryer to 190ºC and spray with a little oil
2. Meanwhile, take your bread and cut a hole into the middle of each piece
3. Place one slice inside your fryer and crack one egg into the middle
4. Season with a little salt and pepper
5. Cook for 5 minutes, before turning over and cooking for a further 2 minutes
6. Remove the first slice and repeat the process with the remaining slice of bread and egg

Monte Cristo Breakfast Sandwich

Servings: 4 | Cooking Time:xx

Ingredients:

- 1 egg
- 2 slices of sandwich bread
- 1/4 tsp vanilla extract
- 4 slices of sliced Swiss cheese
- 4 slices of sliced deli ham
- 4 slices of sliced turkey
- 1 tsp melted butter
- Powdered sugar for serving

Directions:

1. In a small bowl, mix together the egg and vanilla extract, combining well
2. Take your bread and assemble your sandwich, starting with a slice of cheese, then the ham, turkey, and then another slice of the cheese, with the other slice of bread on the top
3. Compress the sandwich a little, so it cooks better
4. Take a piece of cooking foil and brush over it with the butter
5. Take your sandwich and dip each side into the egg mixture, leaving it to one side for around half a minute
6. Place the sandwich on the foil and place it inside your fryer
7. Cook at 200ºC for around 10 minutes, before turning the sandwich over and cooking for another 8 minutes
8. Transfer your sandwich onto a plate and sprinkle with a little powdered sugar

Sweet Potato Fries

Servings: 4 | Cooking Time:xx

Ingredients:

- 2 medium sweet potatoes
- 2 teaspoons olive oil
- ½ teaspoon salt
- ½ teaspoon chilli/hot red pepper flakes
- ½ teaspoon smoked paprika

Directions:

1. Preheat the air-fryer to 190ºC/375ºF.
2. Peel the sweet potatoes and slice into fries about 1 x 1 cm/½ x ½ in. by the length of the potato. Toss the sweet potato fries in the oil, salt, chilli and paprika, making sure every fry is coated.
3. Tip into the preheated air-fryer in a single layer (you may need to cook them in two batches, depending on the size of your air-fryer). Air-fry for 10 minutes, turning once halfway during cooking. Serve immediately.

French Toast Slices

Servings: 1 | Cooking Time:xx

Ingredients:

- 2 eggs
- 5 slices sandwich bread
- 100ml milk
- 2 tbsp flour
- 3 tbsp sugar
- 1 tsp ground cinnamon
- 1/2 tsp vanilla extract
- Pinch of salt

Directions:

1. Preheat your air fryer to 220ºC
2. Take your bread and cut it into three pieces of the same size
3. Take a mixing bowl and combine the other ingredients until smooth
4. Dip the bread into the mixture, coating evenly
5. Take a piece of parchment paper and lay it inside the air fryer
6. Arrange the bread on the parchment paper in one layer
7. Cook for 5 minutes
8. Turn and cook for another 5 minutes

Mexican Breakfast Burritos

Servings: 6 | Cooking Time:xx

Ingredients:

- 6 scrambled eggs
- 6 medium tortillas
- Half a minced red pepper
- 8 sausages, cut into cubes and browned
- 4 pieces of bacon, pre-cooked and cut into pieces
- 65g grated cheese of your choice
- A small amount of olive oil for cooking

Directions:

1. Into a regular mixing bowl, combine the eggs, bell pepper, bacon pieces, the cheese, and the browned sausage, giving everything a good stir
2. Take your first tortilla and place half a cup of the mixture into the middle, folding up the top and bottom and rolling closed
3. Repeat until all your tortillas have been used
4. Arrange the burritos into the bottom of your fryer and spray with a little oil
5. Cook the burritos at 170ºC for 5 minutes

Sauces & Snack And Appetiser Recipes

Spicy Egg Rolls

Servings: 4 | Cooking Time:xx

Ingredients:

- 1 rotisserie chicken, shredded and diced
- 3 tbsp water
- 3 tbsp taco seasoning
- 1 can of black beans, drained
- 1 red bell pepper, diced
- 1 can of sweetcorn, drained
- 1 jalapeño pepper, deseeded and minced
- 2 packs of egg roll wrappers
- 250g grated strong cheddar cheese
- 250g grated Monterey Jack cheese

Directions:

1. Take a medium bowl and add the water and taco seasoning, combining well
2. Add the shredded check and coat well
3. Lay out an egg roll wrapper and arrange it so that one corner is facing towards you
4. Add 3 tablespoons of the mixture into the wrapper, just below the middle
5. Roll the corner facing you upwards, pulling it tightly closed over the mixture
6. Add a little water to the other two corners and fold into the centre and pat down to seal
7. Roll the rest of the wrapper up, so that all the corners are sealed
8. Repeat with the rest of the mixture
9. Preheat the air fryer to 220ºC
10. Cook for 9 minutes and turn over at the halfway point

Beetroot Crisps

Servings: 2 | Cooking Time:xx

Ingredients:

- 3 medium beetroots
- 2 tbsp oil
- Salt to taste

Directions:

1. Peel and thinly slice the beetroot
2. Coat with the oil and season with salt
3. Preheat the air fryer to 200ºC
4. Place in the air fryer and cook for 12-18 minutes until crispy

Waffle Fries

Servings: 4 | Cooking Time:xx

Ingredients:

- 2 large potatoes, russet potatoes work best
- 1 tsp salt for seasoning
- Waffle cutter

Directions:

1. Peel the potatoes and slice using the waffle cutter. You can also use a mandolin cutter that has a blade
2. Transfer the potatoes to a bowl and season with the salt, coating evenly
3. Add to the air fryer and cook at 220°C for 15 minutes, shaking every so often

Air-fried Pickles

Servings: 4 | Cooking Time:xx

Ingredients:

- 1/2 cup mayonnaise
- 2 tsp sriracha sauce
- 1 jar dill pickle slices
- 1 egg
- 2 tbsp milk
- 50g flour
- 50g cornmeal
- ½ tsp seasoned salt
- ¼ tsp paprika
- ¼ tsp garlic powder
- ⅛ tsp pepper
- Cooking spray

Directions:

1. Mix the mayo and sriracha together in a bowl and set aside
2. Heat the air fryer to 200°C
3. Drain the pickles and pat dry
4. Mix egg and milk together, in another bowl mix all the remaining ingredients
5. Dip the pickles in the egg mix then in the flour mix
6. Spray the air fryer with cooking spray
7. Cook for about 4 minutes until crispy

Tasty Pumpkin Seeds

Servings: 2 | Cooking Time:xx

Ingredients:

- 1 ¾ cups pumpkin seeds
- 2 tsp avocado oil
- 1 tsp paprika
- 1 tsp salt

Directions:

1. Preheat air fryer to 180°C
2. Add all ingredients to a bowl and mix well
3. Place in the air fryer and cook for 35 minutes shaking frequently

Focaccia Bread

Servings: 8 | Cooking Time:xx

Ingredients:

- 500g pizza dough
- 3 tbsp olive oil
- 2-3 garlic cloves, chopped
- ¼ tsp red pepper flakes
- 50g parsley
- 1 tsp basil
- 100g chopped red peppers
- 60g black olives halved
- 60g green olives halved
- Salt and pepper to taste

Directions:

1. Preheat the air fryer to 180ºC, make indentations in the pizza dough with your finger tips and set aside
2. Heat the olive oil in a pan add the garlic and cook for a few minutes, add the remaining ingredients and cook for another 5-8 minutes not letting the oil get too hot
3. Spread the oil mix over the dough with a spatula
4. Place in the air fryer and cook for 12-15 minutes

Scotch Eggs

Servings: 6 | Cooking Time:xx

Ingredients:

- 300g pork sausage
- 6 hard boiled eggs, shelled
- 50g cup flour
- 2 eggs, beaten
- 1 cup breadcrumbs
- Cooking spray

Directions:

1. Divide sausage into 6 portions
2. Place an egg in the middle of each portion and wrap around the egg
3. Dip the sausage in flour, then egg and then coat in breadcrumbs
4. Place in the air fryer and cook at 200ºC for 12 minutes

Mini Calzones

Servings: 16 | Cooking Time:xx

Ingredients:

- Flour for rolling out the dough
- 1 round pizza dough
- 100g pizza sauce

Directions:

1. Roll out the dough to ¼ inch thick
2. Cut out 8-10 dough rounds using a cutter
3. Re-roll the dough and cut out another 6 rounds
4. Top each round with pizza sauce, cheese and pepperoni
5. Fold dough over and pinch the edges to seal
6. Heat the air fryer to 190°C
7. Place the calzone in the air fryer and cook for about 8 minutes until golden brown

Snack Style Falafel

Servings: 15 | Cooking Time:xx

Ingredients:

- 150g dry garbanzo beans
- 300g coriander
- 75g flat leaf parsley
- 1 red onion, quartered
- 1 clove garlic
- 2 tbsp chickpea flour
- Cooking spray
- 1 tbsp cumin
- 1 tbsp coriander
- 1 tbsp sriracha
- ½ tsp baking powder
- Salt and pepper to taste
- ¼ tsp baking soda

Directions:

1. Add all ingredients apart from the baking soda and baking powder to a food processor and blend well
2. Cover and rest for 1 hour
3. Heat air fryer to 190°C
4. Add baking powder and baking soda to mix and combine
5. Form mix into 15 equal balls
6. Spray air fryer with cooking spray
7. Add to air fryer and cook for 8-10 minutes

Bacon Smokies

Servings: 8 | Cooking Time:xx

Ingredients:

- 150g little smokies (pieces)
- 150g bacon
- 50g brown sugar
- Toothpicks

Directions:

1. Cut the bacon strips into thirds
2. Put the brown sugar into a bowl
3. Coat the bacon with the sugar
4. Wrap the bacon around the little smokies and secure with a toothpick
5. Heat the air fryer to 170°C
6. Place in the air fryer and cook for 10 minutes until crispy

Pretzel Bites

Servings: 2 | Cooking Time:xx

Ingredients:

- 650g flour
- 2.5 tsp active dry yeast
- 260ml hot water
- 1 tsp salt
- 4 tbsp melted butter
- 2 tbsp sugar

Directions:

1. Take a large bowl and add the flour, sugar and salt
2. Take another bowl and combine the hot water and yeast, stirring until the yeast has dissolved
3. Then, add the yeast mixture to the flour mixture and use your hands to combine
4. Knead for 2 minutes
5. Cover the bowl with a kitchen towel for around half an hour
6. Divide the dough into 6 pieces
7. Preheat the air fryer to 260°C
8. Take each section of dough and tear off a piece, rolling it in your hands to create a rope shape, that is around 1" in thickness
9. Cut into 2" strips
10. Place the small dough balls into the air fryer and leave a little space in-between
11. Cook for 6 minutes
12. Once cooked, remove and brush with melted butter and sprinkle salt on top

Pasta Chips

Servings: 2 | Cooking Time:xx

Ingredients:
- 300g dry pasta bows
- 1 tbsp olive oil
- 1 tbsp nutritional yeast
- 1½ tsp Italian seasoning
- ½ tsp salt

Directions:
1. Cook the pasta for half the time stated on the packet
2. Drain and mix with the oil, yeast, seasoning and salt
3. Place in the air fryer and cook at 200ºC for 5 minutes shake and cook for a further 3 minutes until crunchy

Thai Bites

Servings: 4 | Cooking Time:xx

Ingredients:
- 400g pork mince
- 1 onion
- 1 tsp garlic paste
- 1 tbsp soy
- 1 tbsp Worcester sauce
- Salt and pepper
- 2 tsp Thai curry paste
- ½ lime juice and zest
- 1 tsp mixed spice
- 1 tsp Chinese spice
- 1 tsp coriander

Directions:
1. Place all ingredients in a bowl and mix well
2. Shape into balls
3. Place in the air fryer and cook at 180ºC for 15 minutes

Jalapeño Poppers

Servings: 2 | Cooking Time:xx

Ingredients:
- 10 jalapeños, halved and deseeded
- 100g cream cheese
- 50g parsley
- 150g breadcrumbs

Directions:
1. Mix 1/2 the breadcrumbs with the cream cheese
2. Add the parsley
3. Stuff the peppers with the cream cheese mix
4. Top the peppers with the remaining breadcrumbs
5. Heat the air fryer to 185ºC
6. Place in the air fryer and cook for 6-8 minutes

Pepperoni Bread

Servings: 4 | Cooking Time:xx

Ingredients:

- Cooking spray
- 400g pizza dough
- 200g pepperoni
- 1 tbsp dried oregano
- Ground pepper to taste
- Garlic salt to taste
- 1 tsp melted butter
- 1 tsp grated parmesan
- 50g grated mozzarella

Directions:

1. Line a baking tin with 2 inch sides with foil to fit in the air fryer
2. Spray with cooking spray
3. Preheat the air fryer to 200°C
4. Roll the pizza dough into 1 inch balls and line the baking tin
5. Sprinkle with pepperoni, oregano, pepper and garlic salt
6. Brush with melted butter and sprinkle with parmesan
7. Place in the air fryer and cook for 15 minutes
8. Sprinkle with mozzarella and cook for another 2 minutes

Peppers With Aioli Dip

Servings: 4 | Cooking Time:xx

Ingredients:

- 250g shishito peppers
- 2 tsp avocado oil
- 5 tbsp mayonnaise
- 2 tbsp lemon juice
- 1 minced clove of garlic
- 1 tbsp chopped parsley
- Salt and pepper for seasoning

Directions:

1. Take a medium bowl and combine the mayonnaise with the lemon juice, garlic, parsley and seasoning and create a smooth dip
2. Preheat the air fryer to 220°C
3. Toss the peppers in the oil and add to the air fryer
4. Cook for 4 minutes, until the peppers are soft and blistered on the outside
5. Remove and serve with the dip

Corn Nuts

Servings: 8 | Cooking Time:xx

Ingredients:

- 1 giant white corn
- 3 tbsp vegetable oil
- 2 tsp salt

Directions:

1. Place the corn in a large bowl, cover with water and sit for 8 hours
2. Drain, pat dry and air dry for 20 minutes
3. Preheat the air fryer to 200ºC
4. Place in a bowl and coat with oil and salt
5. Cook in the air fryer for 10 minutes shake then cook for a further 10 minutes

Sweet Potato Crisps

Servings: 4 | Cooking Time:xx

Ingredients:

- 1 sweet potato, peeled and thinly sliced
- 2 tbsp oil
- ¼ tsp salt
- ¼ tsp pepper
- 1 tsp chopped rosemary
- Cooking spray

Directions:

1. Place all ingredients in a bowl and mix well
2. Place in the air fryer and cook at 175ºC for about 15 minutes until crispy

Salt And Vinegar Chips

Servings: 4 | Cooking Time:xx

Ingredients:

- 6-10 Jerusalem artichokes, thinly sliced
- 150ml apple cider vinegar
- 2 tbsp olive oil
- Sea salt

Directions:

1. Soak the artichoke in apple cider vinegar for 20-30 minutes
2. Preheat the air fryer to 200ºC
3. Coat the artichoke in olive oil
4. Place in the air fryer and cook for 15 Minutes
5. Sprinkle with salt

Onion Pakoda

Servings: 2 | Cooking Time:xx

Ingredients:

- 200g gram flour
- 2 onions, thinly sliced
- 1 tbsp crushed coriander seeds
- 1 tsp chilli powder
- ¾ tsp salt
- ¼ tsp turmeric
- ¼ tsp baking soda

Directions:

1. Mix all the ingredients together in a large bowl
2. Make bite sized pakodas
3. Heat the air fryer to 200ºC
4. Line the air fryer with foil
5. Place the pakoda in the air fryer and cook for 5 minutes
6. Turn over and cook for a further 5 minutes

Poultry Recipes

Healthy Bang Bang Chicken

Servings: 4 | Cooking Time:xx

Ingredients:

- 500g chicken breasts, cut into pieces of around 1" in size
- 1 beaten egg
- 50ml milk
- 1 tbsp hot pepper sauce
- 80g flour
- 70g tapioca starch
- 1 ½ tsp seasoned starch
- 1 tsp garlic granules
- ½ tsp cumin
- 6 tbsp plain Greek yogurt
- 3 tbsp sweet chilli sauce
- 1 tsp hot sauce

Directions:

1. Preheat the air fryer to 190ºC
2. Take a mixing bowl and combine the egg, milk and hot sauce
3. Take another bowl and combine the flour, tapioca starch, salt, garlic and cumin
4. Dip the chicken pieces into the sauce bowl and then into the flour bowl
5. Place the chicken into the air fryer
6. Whilst cooking, mix together the Greek yogurt, sweet chilli sauce and hot sauce and serve with the chicken

Chicken Tikka

Servings: 2 | Cooking Time:xx

Ingredients:

- 2 chicken breasts, diced
- FIRST MARINADE
- freshly squeezed juice of ½ a lemon
- 1 tablespoon freshly grated ginger
- 1 tablespoon freshly grated garlic
- a good pinch of salt
- SECOND MARINADE
- 100 g/½ cup Greek yogurt
- ½ teaspoon chilli powder
- ½ teaspoon chilli paste
- ½ teaspoon turmeric
- ½ teaspoon garam masala
- 1 tablespoon olive oil

Directions:

1. Mix the ingredients for the first marinade together in a bowl, add in the chicken and stir to coat all the chicken pieces. Leave in the fridge to marinate for 20 minutes.
2. Combine the second marinade ingredients. Once the first marinade has had 20 minutes, add the second marinade to the chicken and stir well. Leave in the fridge for at least 4 hours.
3. Preheat the air-fryer to 180ºC/350ºF.
4. Thread the chicken pieces onto metal skewers that fit in your air-fryer. Add the skewers to the preheated air-fryer and air-fry for 10 minutes. Check the internal temperature of the chicken has reached at least 74ºC/165ºF using a meat thermometer – if not, cook for another few minutes and then serve.

Chicken Jalfrezi

Servings: 4 | Cooking Time:xx

Ingredients:

- 500g chicken breasts
- 1 tbsp water
- 4 tbsp tomato sauce
- 1 chopped onion
- 1 chopped bell pepper
- 2 tsp love oil
- 1 tsp turmeric
- 1 tsp cayenne pepper
- 2 tsp garam masala
- Salt and pepper to taste

Directions:

1. Take a large mixing bowl and add the chicken, onions, pepper, salt, garam masala, turmeric, oil and cayenne pepper, combining well
2. Place the chicken mix in the air fryer and cook at 180°C for 15 minutes
3. Take a microwave-safe bowl and add the tomato sauce, water salt, garam masala and cayenne, combining well
4. Cook in the microwave for 1 minute, stir then cook for a further minute
5. Remove the chicken from the air fryer and pour the sauce over the top.
6. Serve whilst still warm

Crunchy Chicken Tenders

Servings: 4 | Cooking Time:xx

Ingredients:

- 8 regular chicken tenders (frozen work best)
- 1 egg
- 2 tbsp olive oil
- 150g dried breadcrumbs

Directions:

1. Heat the fryer to 175°C
2. In a small bowl, beat the egg
3. In another bowl, combine the oil and the breadcrumbs together
4. Take one tender and first dip it into the egg, and then cover it in the breadcrumb mixture
5. Place the tender into the fryer basket
6. Repeat with the rest of the tenders, arranging them carefully so they don't touch inside the basket
7. Cook for 12 minutes, checking that they are white in the centre before serving

Chicken Tikka Masala

Servings: 4 | Cooking Time:xx

Ingredients:

- 100g tikka masala curry pasta
- 200g low fat yogurt
- 600g skinless chicken breasts
- 1 tbsp vegetable oil
- 1 onion, chopped
- 400g can of the whole, peeled tomatoes
- 20ml water
- 1 tbsp sugar
- 2 tbsp lemon juice
- 1 small bunch of chopped coriander leaves

Directions:

1. Take a bowl and combine the tikka masala curry paste with half the yogurt
2. Cut the chicken into strips
3. Preheat the air fryer to 200ºC
4. Add the yogurt mixture and coat the chicken until fully covered
5. Place into the refrigerator for 2 hours
6. Place the oil and onion in the air fryer and cook for 10 minutes
7. Add the marinated chicken, tomatoes, water and the rest of the yogurt and combine
8. Add the sugar and lemon juice and combine again
9. Cook for 15 minutes

Thai Turkey Burgers

Servings: 4 | Cooking Time:xx

Ingredients:

- 1 courgette/zucchini, about 200 g/7 oz.
- 400 g/14 oz. minced/ground turkey breast
- 35 g/½ cup fresh breadcrumbs (gluten-free if you wish)
- 1 teaspoon Thai 7 spice seasoning
- 1 teaspoon salt
- 1 teaspoon olive oil

Directions:

1. Coarsely grate the courgette/zucchini, then place in a piece of muslin/cheesecloth and squeeze out the water. Combine the grated courgette with all other ingredients except the olive oil, mixing together well. Divide the mixture into 4 equal portions and mould into burgers. Brush with oil.
2. Preheat the air-fryer to 190ºC/375ºC.
3. Add the turkey burgers to the preheated air-fryer and air-fry for 15 minutes, turning once halfway through cooking. Check the internal temperature of the burgers has reached at least 74ºC/165ºF using a meat thermometer – if not, cook for another few minutes and then serve.

Orange Chicken

Servings: 2 | Cooking Time:xx

Ingredients:

- 600g chicken thighs, boneless and skinless
- 2 tbsp cornstarch
- 60ml orange juice
- 1 tbsp soy sauce
- 2 tbsp brown sugar
- 1 tbsp rice wine vinegar
- 1/4 teaspoon ground ginger
- Pinch of red pepper flakes
- Zest of one orange
- 2 tsp water and 2 tsp cornstarch mixed together

Directions:

1. Preheat your air fryer to 250°C
2. Take a bowl and combine the chicken with the cornstarch
3. Place in the air fryer and cook for 9 minutes
4. Take a bowl and combine the rest of the ingredients, except for the water and cornstarch mixture
5. Place in a saucepan and bring to the boil and then turn down to a simmer for 5 minutes
6. Add the water and cornstarch mixture to the pan and combine well
7. Remove the chicken from the fryer and pour the sauce over the top

Keto Tandoori Chicken

Servings: 2 | Cooking Time:xx

Ingredients:

- 500g chicken tenders, halved
- 1 tbsp minced ginger
- 1 tbsp minced garlic
- 1 tsp cayenne pepper
- 1 tsp turmeric
- 1 tsp garam masala
- 60ml yogurt
- 25g coriander leaves
- Salt and pepper to taste

Directions:

1. Take a large mixing bowl and combine all the ingredients, except the chicken
2. Once combined, add the chicken to the bowl and make sure it is fully coated
3. Preheat the air fryer to 160°C
4. Place the chicken in the air fryer and baste with oil
5. Cook for 10 minutes, turning over and then cooking for another 5 minutes
6. Serve whilst still warm

Nashville Chicken

Servings: 4 | Cooking Time:xx

Ingredients:

- 400g boneless chicken breast tenders
- 2 tsp salt
- 2 tsp coarsely ground black pepper
- 2 tbsp hot sauce
- 2 tbsp pickle juice
- 500g all purpose flour
- 3 large eggs
- 300ml buttermilk
- 2 tbsp olive oil
- 6 tbsp cayenne pepper
- 3 tbsp dark brown sugar
- 1 tsp chilli powder
- 1 tsp garlic powder
- 1 tsp paprika
- Salt and pepper to taste

Directions:

1. Take a large mixing bowl and add the chicken, hot sauce, pickle juice, salt and pepper and combine
2. Place in the refrigerator for 3 hours
3. Transfer the flour to a bowl
4. Take another bowl and add the eggs, buttermilk and 1 tbsp of the hot sauce, combining well
5. Press each piece of chicken into the flour and coat well
6. Place the chicken into the buttermilk mixture and then back into the flour
7. Allow to sit or 10 minutes
8. Preheat the air fryer to 193C
9. Whisk together the spices, brown sugar and olive oil to make the sauce and pour over the chicken tenders
10. Serve whilst still warm

Chicken Balls, Greek-style

Servings: 4 | Cooking Time:xx

Ingredients:

- 500g ground chicken
- 1 egg
- 1 tbsp dried oregano
- 1.5 tbsp garlic paste
- 1 tsp lemon zest
- 1 tsp dried onion powder
- Salt and pepper to taste

Directions:

1. Take a bowl and combine all ingredients well
2. Use your hands to create meatballs - you should be able to make 12 balls
3. Preheat your air fryer to 260ºC
4. Add the meatballs to the fryer and cook for 9 minutes

Chicken Fajitas

Servings: 3 | Cooking Time:xx

Ingredients:

- 2 boneless chicken breasts, sliced into strips
- 5 mini (bell) peppers, sliced into strips
- 1 courgette/zucchini, sliced into 5-mm/¼-in. thick discs
- 2 tablespoons olive oil
- 28-g/1-oz. packet fajita seasoning mix
- TO SERVE
- wraps
- sliced avocado
- chopped tomato and red onion
- grated Red Leicester cheese
- plain yogurt
- coriander/cilantro
- lime wedges, for squeezing

Directions:

1. Combine the chicken, (bell) peppers, courgettes/zucchini and olive oil in a bowl. Add the fajita seasoning and stir to coat.
2. Preheat the air-fryer to 180°C/350°F.
3. Add the coated vegetables and chicken to the preheated air-fryer and air-fry for 12 minutes, shaking the drawer a couple of times during cooking. Check the internal temperature of the chicken has reached at least 74°C/165°F using a meat thermometer – if not, cook for another few minutes.
4. Serve immediately alongside the serving suggestions or your own choices of accompaniments.

Honey Cajun Chicken Thighs

Servings: 6 | Cooking Time:xx

Ingredients:

- 100ml buttermilk
- 1 tsp hot sauce
- 400g skinless, boneless chicken thighs
- 150g all purpose flour
- 60g tapioca flour
- 2.5 tsp cajun seasoning
- ½ tsp garlic salt
- ½ tsp honey powder
- ¼ tsp ground paprika
- ⅛ tsp cayenne pepper
- 4 tsp honey

Directions:

1. Take a large bowl and combine the buttermilk and hot sauce
2. Transfer to a plastic bag and add the chicken thighs
3. Allow to marinate for 30 minutes
4. Take another bowl and add the flour, tapioca flour, cajun seasoning, garlic, salt, honey powder, paprika, and cayenne pepper, combining well
5. Dredge the chicken through the mixture
6. Preheat the air fryer to 175C
7. Cook for 15 minutes before flipping the thighs over and cooking for another 10 minutes
8. Drizzle 1 tsp of honey over each thigh

Hawaiian Chicken

Servings: 2 | Cooking Time:xx

Ingredients:

- 2 chicken breasts
- 1 tbsp butter
- A pinch of salt and pepper
- 160ml pineapple juice
- 25g brown sugar
- 3 tbsp soy sauce
- 2 tsp water
- 1 clove of garlic, minced
- 1 tsp grated ginger
- 2 tsp cornstarch

Directions:

1. Preheat the air fryer to 260°C
2. Take a bowl and combine the butter and salt and pepper
3. Cover the chicken with the butter and cook in the fryer for 15 minutes, turning halfway
4. Remove and allow to rest for 5 minutes
5. Take another bowl and mix together the pineapple juice, soy sauce, garlic, ginger, and brown sugar
6. Transfer to a saucepan and simmer for 5 minutes
7. Combine the water and cornstarch and add to the sauce, stirring continually for another minute
8. Slice the chicken into strips and pour the sauce over the top

Air Fryer Chicken Thigh Schnitzel

Servings: 4 | Cooking Time:xx

Ingredients:

- 300g boneless chicken thighs
- 160g seasoned breadcrumbs
- 1 tsp salt
- ½ tsp ground black pepper
- 30g flour
- 1 egg
- Cooking spray

Directions:

1. Lay the chicken on a sheet of parchment paper and add another on top
2. Use a mallet or a rolling pin to flatten it down
3. Take a bowl and add the breadcrumbs with the salt and pepper
4. Place the flour into another bowl
5. Dip the chicken into the flour, then the egg, and then the breadcrumbs
6. Preheat air fryer to 190°C
7. Place the chicken into the air fryer and spray with cooking oil
8. Cook for 6 minutes

Air Fried Maple Chicken Thighs

Servings: 4 | Cooking Time:xx

Ingredients:

- 200ml buttermilk
- ½ tbsp maple syrup
- 1 egg
- 1 tsp granulated garlic salt
- 4 chicken thighs with the bone in
- 140g all purpose flour
- 65g tapioca flour
- 1 tsp sweet paprika
- 1 tsp onion powder
- ¼ tsp ground black pepper
- ¼ tsp cayenne pepper
- ½ tsp granulated garlic
- ½ tsp honey powder

Directions:

1. Take a bowl and combine the buttermilk, maple syrup, egg and garlic powder
2. Transfer to a bag and add chicken thighs, shaking to combine well
3. Set aside for 1 hour
4. Take a shallow bowl and add the flour, tapioca flour, salt, sweet paprika, smoked paprika, pepper, cayenne pepper and honey powder, combining well
5. Preheat the air fryer to 190°C
6. Drag the chicken through flour mixture and place the chicken skin side down in the air fryer Cook for 12 minutes, until white in the middle

Buffalo Chicken Wontons

Servings: 6 | Cooking Time:xx

Ingredients:

- 200g shredded chicken
- 1 tbsp buffalo sauce
- 4 tbsp softened cream cheese
- 1 sliced spring onion
- 2 tbsp blue cheese crumbles
- 12 wonton wrappers

Directions:

1. Preheat the air fryer to 200°C
2. Take a bowl and combine the chicken and buffalo sauce
3. In another bowl mix the cream cheese until a smooth consistency has formed and then combine the scallion blue cheese and seasoned chicken
4. Take the wonton wrappers and run wet fingers along each edge
5. Place 1 tbsp of the filling into the centre of the wonton and fold the corners together
6. Cook at 200°C for 3 to 5 minutes, until golden brown

Pizza Chicken Nuggets

Servings: 2 | Cooking Time:xx

Ingredients:

- 60 g/¾ cup dried breadcrumbs (see page 9)
- 20 g/¼ cup grated Parmesan
- ½ teaspoon dried oregano
- ¼ teaspoon freshly ground black pepper
- 150 g/⅔ cup Mediterranean sauce (see page 102) or 150 g/5½ oz. jarred tomato pasta sauce (keep any leftover sauce for serving)
- 400 g/14 oz. chicken fillets

Directions:

1. Preheat the air-fryer to 180°C/350°F.
2. Combine the breadcrumbs, Parmesan, oregano and pepper in a bowl. Have the Mediterranean or pasta sauce in a separate bowl.
3. Dip each chicken fillet in the tomato sauce first, then roll in the breadcrumb mix until coated fully.
4. Add the breaded fillets to the preheated air-fryer and air-fry for 10 minutes. Check the internal temperature of the chicken has reached at least 74°C/165°F using a meat thermometer – if not, cook for another few minutes.
5. Serve with some additional sauce that has been warmed through.

Chicken Fried Rice

Servings: 4 | Cooking Time:xx

Ingredients:

- 400g cooked white rice
- 400g cooked chicken, diced
- 200g frozen peas and carrots
- 6 tbsp soy sauce
- 1 tbsp vegetable oil
- 1 diced onion

Directions:

1. Take a large bowl and add the rice, vegetable oil and soy sauce and combine well
2. Add the frozen peas, carrots, diced onion and the chicken and mix together well
3. Pour the mixture into a nonstick pan
4. Place the pan into the air fryer
5. Cook at 182C for 20 minutes

Turkey Cutlets In Mushroom Sauce

Servings: 2 | Cooking Time:xx

Ingredients:

- 2 turkey cutlets
- 1 tbsp butter
- 1 can of cream of mushroom sauce
- 160ml milk
- Salt and pepper for seasoning

Directions:

1. Preheat the air fryer to 220ºC
2. Brush the turkey cults with the butter and seasoning
3. Place in the air fryer and cook for 11 minutes
4. Add the mushroom soup and milk to a pan and cook over the stone for around 10 minutes, stirring every so often
5. Top the turkey cutlets with the sauce

Chicken And Wheat Stir Fry

Servings: 4 | Cooking Time:xx

Ingredients:

- 1 onion
- 1 clove of garlic
- 200g skinless boneless chicken breast halves
- 3 whole tomatoes
- 400ml water
- 1 chicken stock cube
- 1 tbsp curry powder
- 130g wheat berries
- 1 tbsp vegetable oil

Directions:

1. Thinly slice the onion and garlic
2. Chop the chicken and tomatoes into cubes
3. Take a large saucepan and add the water, chicken stock, curry powder and wheat berries, combining well
4. Pour the oil into the air fryer bowl and heat for 5 minutes at 200ºC
5. Add the remaining ingredients and pour the contents into the air fryer
6. Cook for 15 minutes

Beef & Lamb And Pork Recipes

Steak Popcorn Bites

Servings: 4 | Cooking Time:xx

Ingredients:

- 500g steak, cut into 1" sized cubes
- 500g potato chips, ridged ones work best
- 100g flour
- 2 beaten eggs
- Salt and pepper to taste

Directions:

1. Place the chips into the food processor and pulse unit you get fine chip crumbs
2. Take a bowl and combine the flour with salt and pepper
3. Add the chips to another bowl and the beaten egg to another bowl
4. Take the steak cubes and dip first in the flour, then the egg and then the chip crumbs
5. Preheat your air fryer to 260°C
6. Place the steak pieces into the fryer and cook for 9 minutes

Hamburgers

Servings: 4 | Cooking Time:xx

Ingredients:

- 500g minced beef
- 1 grated onion
- Salt and pepper to taste

Directions:

1. Preheat air fryer to 200°C
2. Place the grated onion and the beef into a bowl and combine together well
3. Divide minced beef into 4 equal portions, form into patties
4. Season with salt and pepper
5. Place in the air fryer and cook for 10 minutes, turnover and cook for a further 3 minutes

Char Siu Buffalo

Servings: 2 | Cooking Time:xx

Ingredients:

- 1 kg beef, cut into strips
- 4 tbsp honey
- 2 tbsp sugar
- 2 tbsp char siu sauce
- 2 tbsp oyster sauce
- 2 tbsp soy sauce
- 2 tbsp olive oil
- 2 tsp minced garlic
- ¼ tsp bi carbonate of soda

Directions:

1. Place all the ingredients in a bowl, mix well and marinate over night
2. Line the air fryer with foil, add the beef, keep the marinade to one side
3. Cook at 200°C for 10 minutes
4. Brush the pork with the sauce and cook for another 20 minutes at 160°C
5. Remove the meat and set aside
6. Strain the marinade into a saucepan, heat until it thickens
7. Drizzle over the pork and serve with rice

Buttermilk Pork Chops

Servings: 4 | Cooking Time:xx

Ingredients:

- 4 pork chops
- 3 tbsp buttermilk
- 75g flour
- Cooking oil spray
- 1 packet of pork rub
- Salt and pepper to taste

Directions:

1. Rub the chops with the pork rub
2. Place the pork chops in a bowl and drizzle with buttermilk
3. Coat the chops with flour
4. Place in the air fryer and cook at 190°C for 15 minutes turning halfway

Steak Dinner

Servings: 5 | Cooking Time:xx

Ingredients:

- 400g sirloin steak, cut into cubes
- 300g red potatoes, cubed
- 1 pepper
- 1 tsp dried parsley
- ½ tsp pepper
- 2 tsp olive oil
- 1 sliced onion
- 300g chopped mushrooms
- 2 tsp garlic salt
- 2 tsp salt
- 5 tsp butter

Directions:

1. Preheat the air fryer to 200ºC
2. Take 5 pieces of foil, layer meat onion, potatoes, mushrooms and pepper in each one
3. Add 1 tsp of butter to each one
4. Mix seasonings and sprinkle over the top
5. Fold the foil and cook for 25-30 minutes

Beef Bulgogi Burgers

Servings: 4 | Cooking Time:xx

Ingredients:

- 500g minced beef
- 2 tbsp gochujang
- 1 tbsp soy
- 2 tsp minced garlic
- 2 tsp minced ginger
- 2 tsp sugar
- 1 tbsp olive oil
- 1 chopped onion

Directions:

1. Mix all the ingredients in a large bowl, allow to rest for at least 30 minutes in the fridge
2. Divide the meat into four and form into patties
3. Place in the air fryer and cook at 180ºC for about 10 minutes
4. Serve in burger buns, if desired

Salt And Pepper Belly Pork

Servings: 4 | Cooking Time:xx

Ingredients:

- 500g belly pork
- 1 tsp pepper
- ½ tsp salt

Directions:

1. Cut the pork into bite size pieces and season with salt and pepper
2. Heat the air fryer to 200ºC
3. Place in the air fryer and cook for 15 minutes until crisp

Tender Ham Steaks

Servings: 1 | Cooking Time:xx

Ingredients:

- 1 ham steak
- 2 tbsp brown sugar
- 1 tsp honey
- 2 tbsp melted butter

Directions:

1. Preheat the air fryer to 220ºC
2. Combine the melted butter and brown sugar until smooth
3. Add the ham to the air fryer and brush both sides with the butter mixture
4. Cook for 12 minutes, turning halfway through and re-brushing the ham
5. Drizzle honey on top before serving

Mustard Pork Tenderloin

Servings: 2 | Cooking Time:xx

Ingredients:

- 1 pork tenderloin
- 3 tbsp soy sauce
- 2 minced garlic cloves
- 3 tbsp olive oil
- 2 tbsp brown sugar
- 1 tbsp dijon mustard
- Salt and pepper for seasoning

Directions:

1. Take a bowl and combine the ingredients, except for the pork
2. Pour the mixture into a ziplock bag and then add the pork
3. Close the top and make sure the pork is well covered
4. Place in the refrigerator for 30minutes
5. Preheat your air fryer to 260ºC
6. Remove the pork from the bag and place in the fryer
7. Cook for 25 minutes, turning halfway
8. Remove and rest for 5 minutes before slicing into pieces

Beef Wellington

Servings: 4 | Cooking Time:xx

Ingredients:

- 300g chicken liver pate
- 500g shortcrust pastry
- 600g beef fillet
- 1 egg beaten
- Salt and pepper

Directions:

1. Remove all the visible fat from the beef season with salt and pepper. Wrap in cling film and place in the fridge for 1 hour
2. Roll out the pastry, brush the edges with egg
3. Spread the pate over the pastry. Remove the clingfilm from the beef and place in the center of the pastry
4. Seal the pastry around the meat
5. Place in the air fryer and cook at 160°C for 35 minutes

Steak Fajitas

Servings: 4 | Cooking Time:xx

Ingredients:

- 500g sliced steak
- 25g pineapple juice
- 2 tbsp lime juice
- 1 tbsp olive oil
- 1 tbsp soy sauce
- 1 tbsp minced garlic
- ½ tbsp chilli powder
- 1/2 tsp paprika
- 1 tsp cumin
- 1 pepper
- 1 onion
- Salt and pepper to taste

Directions:

1. Mix pineapple juice, lime juice, olive oil, soy sauce, garlic, cumin chilli powder and paprika. Pour over the steak and marinate for 4 hours
2. Line the air fryer with foil, add the peppers and onions, season with salt and pepper
3. Cook at 200°C for 10 minutes, add the steak and cook for another 7 minutes
4. Serve with tortillas
5. Set your fryer to 170°C and cook the sandwich for 4 minutes
6. Turn the sandwich over and cook for another 3 minutes
7. Turn the sandwich out and serve whilst hot
8. Repeat with the other remaining sandwich

Sausage Gnocchi One Pot

Servings: 2 | Cooking Time:xx

Ingredients:

- 4 links of sausage
- 250g green beans, washed and cut into halves
- 1 tsp Italian seasoning
- 1 tbsp olive oil
- 300g gnocchi
- Salt and pepper for seasoning

Directions:

1. Preheat the air fryer to 220ºC
2. Cut the sausage up into pieces
3. Take a bowl and add the gnocchi and green beans, along with the oil and season
4. Place the sausage into the fryer first and then the rest of the ingredients
5. Cook for 12 minutes, giving everything a stir halfway through

Asparagus & Steak Parcels

Servings: 4 | Cooking Time:xx

Ingredients:

- 500g flank steak, cut into 6 equal pieces
- 75ml Tamari sauce
- 2 crushed garlic cloves
- 250g trimmed asparagus
- 3 large bell peppers, thinly sliced
- 2 tbsp butter
- Salt and pepper to taste

Directions:

1. Season the steak to your liking
2. Place the meat in a zip top bag and add the Tamari and garlic, sealing the bag closed
3. Make sure the steaks are fully coated in the sauce and leave them in the fright at least 1 hour, but preferably overnight
4. Remove the steaks from the bag and throw the marinade away
5. Place the peppers and sliced asparagus in the centre of each steak piece
6. Roll the steak up and secure in place with a tooth pick
7. Preheat your air fryer to 250ºC
8. Transfer the meat parcels to the air fryer and cook for 5 minutes
9. Allow to rest before serving
10. Melt the butter in a saucepan, over a medium heat, adding the juices from the air fryer
11. Combine well and keep cooking until thickened
12. Pour the sauce over the steak parcels and season to your liking

Jamaican Jerk Pork

Servings: 4 | Cooking Time:xx

Ingredients:

- 400g pork butt cut into 3 pieces
- 100g jerk paste

Directions:

1. Rub the pork with jerk paste and marinate for 4 hours
2. Preheat air fryer to 190°C
3. Place pork in the air fryer and cook for about 20 minutes turning halfway

Pork Belly With Crackling

Servings: 4 | Cooking Time:xx

Ingredients:

- 800g belly pork
- 1 tsp sea salt
- 1 tsp garlic salt
- 2 tsp five spice
- 1 tsp rosemary
- 1 tsp white pepper
- 1 tsp sugar
- Half a lemon

Directions:

1. Cut lines into the meat portion of the belly pork
2. Cook thoroughly in water
3. Allow to air dry for 3 hours
4. Score the skin and prick holes with a fork
5. Rub with the dry rub mix, rub some lemon juice on the skin
6. Place in the air fryer and cook at 160°C for 30 minutes then at 180°C for a further 30 minutes

Beef Kebobs

Servings: 4 | Cooking Time:xx

Ingredients:

- 500g cubed beef
- 25g low fat sour cream
- 2 tbsp soy sauce
- 8 x 6 inch skewers
- 1 bell pepper
- Half an onion

Directions:

1. Mix the sour cream and soy sauce in a bowl, add the cubed beef and marinate for at least 30 minutes
2. Cut the pepper and onion into 1 inch pieces, soak the skewers in water for 10 minutes
3. Thread beef, bell peppers and onion onto skewers
4. Cook in the air fryer at 200°C for 10 minutes turning halfway

Traditional Pork Chops

Servings: 8 | Cooking Time:xx

Ingredients:

- 8 pork chops
- 1 egg
- 100ml milk
- 300g bread crumbs
- 1 packet of dry ranch seasoning mix
- Salt and pepper to taste

Directions:

1. Preheat air fryer to 170°C
2. Beat the egg in a bowl, add the milk season with salt and pepper
3. In another bowl mix the bread crumbs and ranch dressing mix
4. Dip the pork into the egg then cover with breadcrumbs
5. Place in the air fryer and cook for 12 minutes turning half way

Meatloaf

Servings: 2 | Cooking Time:xx

Ingredients:

- 500g minced pork
- 1 egg
- 3 tbsp breadcrumbs
- 2 mushrooms thickly sliced
- 1 tbsp olive oil
- 1 chopped onion
- 1 tbsp chopped thyme
- 1 tsp salt
- Ground black pepper

Directions:

1. Preheat air fryer to 200°C
2. Combine all the ingredients in a bowl
3. Put the mix into a pan and press down firmly, coat with olive oil
4. Place pan in the air fryer and cook for 25 minutes

Meatballs In Tomato Sauce

Servings: 4 | Cooking Time:xx

Ingredients:

- 1 small onion
- 300g minced pork
- 1 tbsp chopped parsley
- 1 tbsp thyme
- 1 egg
- 3 tbsp bread crumbs
- Salt and pepper to taste

Directions:

1. Place all ingredients into a bowl and mix well
2. Shape mixture into 12 meatballs
3. Heat the air fryer to 200°C
4. Place the meatballs into the air fryer and cook for about 7 minutes
5. Tip the meatballs into an oven dish add the tomato sauce and cook for about 5 minutes in the air fryer until warmed through

Pork Chops With Honey

Servings: 6 | Cooking Time:xx

Ingredients:

- 2 ⅔ tbsp honey
- 100g ketchup
- 6 pork chops
- 2 cloves of garlic
- 2 slices mozzarella cheese

Directions:

1. Preheat air fryer to 200°C
2. Mix all the ingredients together in a bowl
3. Add the pork chops, allow to marinate for at least 1 hour
4. Place in the air fryer and cook for about 12 minutes turning halfway

Fish & Seafood Recipes

Lemon Pepper Shrimp

Servings: 2 | Cooking Time:xx

Ingredients:
- ½ tbsp olive oil
- The juice of 1 lemon
- ¼ tsp paprika
- 1 tsp lemon pepper
- ¼ tsp garlic powder
- 400g uncooked shrimp
- 1 sliced lemon

Directions:
1. Preheat air fryer to 200°C
2. Mix olive oil, lemon juice, paprika, lemon pepper and garlic powder. Add the shrimp and mix well
3. Place shrimp in the air fryer and cook for 6-8 minutes until pink and firm.
4. Serve with lemon slices

Air Fryer Mussels

Servings: 2 | Cooking Time:xx

Ingredients:
- 400g mussels
- 1 tbsp butter
- 200ml water
- 1 tsp basil
- 2 tsp minced garlic
- 1 tsp chives
- 1 tsp parsley

Directions:
1. Preheat air fryer to 200°C
2. Clean the mussels, soak for 30 minutes, and remove the beard
3. Add all ingredients to an air fryer-safe pan
4. Cook for 3 minutes
5. Check to see if the mussels have opened, if not cook for a further 2 minutes. Once all mussels are open, they are ready to eat.

Crispy Nacho Prawns

Servings: 6 | Cooking Time:xx

Ingredients:

- 1 egg
- 18 large prawns
- 1 bag of nacho cheese flavoured corn chips, crushed

Directions:

1. Wash the prawns and pat dry
2. Place the chips into a bowl
3. In another bowl, whisk the egg
4. Dip the prawns into the egg and then the nachos
5. Preheat the air fryer to 180ºC
6. Cook for 8 minutes

Salmon Patties

Servings: 4 | Cooking Time:xx

Ingredients:

- 400g salmon
- 1 egg
- 1 diced onion
- 200g breadcrumbs
- 1 tsp dill weed

Directions:

1. Remove all bones and skin from the salmon
2. Mix egg, onion, dill weed and bread crumbs with the salmon
3. Shape mixture into patties and place into the air fryer
4. Set air fryer to 180ºC
5. Cook for 5 minutes then turn them over and cook for a further 5 minutes until golden brown

Air Fried Scallops

Servings: 2 | Cooking Time:xx

Ingredients:

- 6 scallops
- 1 tbsp olive oil
- Salt and pepper to taste

Directions:

1. Brush the filets with olive oil
2. Sprinkle with salt and pepper
3. Place in the air fryer and cook at 200ºC for 2 mins
4. Turn the scallops over and cook for another 2 minutes

Store-cupboard Fishcakes

Servings: 3 | Cooking Time:xx

Ingredients:

- 400 g/14 oz. cooked potato – either mashed potato or the insides of jacket potatoes (see page 124)
- 2 x 150–200-g/5½–7-oz. cans fish, such as tuna or salmon, drained
- 2 eggs
- ¾ teaspoon salt
- 1 teaspoon dried parsley
- ½ teaspoon freshly ground black pepper
- 1 tablespoon olive oil
- caper dressing (see page 79), to serve

Directions:

1. Mix the cooked potato, fish, eggs, salt, parsley and pepper together in a bowl, then divide into 6 equal portions and form into fishcakes. Drizzle the olive oil over both sides of each fishcake.
2. Preheat the air-fryer to 180°C/350°F.
3. Add the fishcakes to the preheated air-fryer and air-fry for 15 minutes, turning halfway through cooking. Serve with salad and tartare sauce or Caper Dressing.

Tandoori Salmon

Servings: 4 | Cooking Time:xx

Ingredients:

- 300g salmon
- 1 tbsp butter
- 1 tbsp tandoori spice
- Salt and pepper to taste
- 1 small tomato
- Half a red onion
- 600g plain yogurt
- 30 fresh mint leaves, chopped
- 1 tsp minced green chilli
- 1 tbsp ground cumin
- Half a cucumber, chopped

Directions:

1. Cut the salmon into cubes and coat in the tandoori spice mix. Chill for 30 minutes to marinate
2. Blend mint, cumin and chilli with ¼ of the yogurt refrigerate and leave to steep
3. Peel the tomato and cut into cubes. Peel the cucumber and chop into cubes, finely dice the onion
4. Cook the salmon in the air fryer for 5-6 minutes at 200°C
5. Mix the flavoured yogurt with the remaining yogurt, tomato, cucumber and onion
6. Place the sauce in serving bowls and place the salmon on top

Crunchy Fish

Servings: 4 | Cooking Time:xx

Ingredients:

- 200g dry breadcrumbs
- 4 tbsp olive oil
- 4 fillets of white fish
- 1 beaten egg
- 1 sliced lemon

Directions:

1. Heat the fryer to 180ºC
2. In a medium mixing bowl, combine the olive oil and the breadcrumbs
3. Take the fish and first dip it into the egg and then the breadcrumbs, making sure they are evenly coated well
4. Arrange the fish into the basket
5. Cook for 12 minutes
6. Remove and serve with lemon slices

Garlic Butter Salmon

Servings: 2 | Cooking Time:xx

Ingredients:

- 2 salmon fillets, boneless with the skin left on
- 1 tsp minced garlic
- 2 tbsp melted butter
- 1 tsp chopped parsley
- Salt and pepper to taste

Directions:

1. Preheat the air fryer to 270 ºC
2. Take a bowl and combine the melted butter, parsley and garlic to create a sauce
3. Season the salmon to your liking
4. Brush the salmon with the garlic mixture, on both sides
5. Place the salmon into the fryer, with the skin side facing down
6. Cook for 10 minutes - the salmon is done when it flakes with ease

Shrimp With Yum Yum Sauce

Servings: 4 | Cooking Time:xx

Ingredients:
- 400g peeled jumbo shrimp
- 1 tbsp soy sauce
- 1 tbsp garlic paste
- 1 tbsp ginger paste
- 4 tbsp mayo
- 2 tbsp ketchup
- 1 tbsp sugar
- 1 tsp paprika
- 1 tsp garlic powder

Directions:
1. Mix soy sauce, garlic paste and ginger paste in a bowl. Add the shrimp, allow to marinate for 15 minutes
2. In another bowl mix ketchup, mayo, sugar, paprika and the garlic powder to make the yum yum sauce.
3. Set the air fryer to 200ºC, place shrimp in the basket and cook for 8-10 minutes

Coconut Shrimp

Servings: 4 | Cooking Time:xx

Ingredients:
- 250g flour
- 1 ½ tsp black pepper
- 2 eggs
- 150g unsweetened flaked coconut
- 1 Serrano chilli, thinly sliced
- 25g panko bread crumbs
- 300g shrimp raw
- ½ tsp salt
- 4 tbsp honey
- 25ml lime juice

Directions:
1. Mix together flour and pepper, in another bowl beat the eggs and in another bowl mix the panko and coconut
2. Dip each of the shrimp in the flour mix then the egg and then cover in the coconut mix
3. Coat the shrimp in cooking spray
4. Place in the air fryer and cook at 200ºC for 6-8 mins turning half way through
5. Mix together the honey, lime juice and chilli and serve with the shrimp

Honey Sriracha Salmon

Servings: 2 | Cooking Time:xx

Ingredients:

- 25g sriracha
- 25g honey
- 500g salmon fillets
- 1 tbsp soy sauce

Directions:

1. Mix the honey, soy sauce and sriracha, keep half the mix to one side for dipping
2. Place the salmon in the sauce skin side up and marinade for 30 minutes
3. Spray air fryer basket with cooking spray
4. Heat the air fryer to 200°C
5. Place salmon in the air fryer skin side down and cook for 12 minutes

Copycat Fish Fingers

Servings: 2 | Cooking Time:xx

Ingredients:

- 2 slices wholemeal bread, grated into breadcrumbs
- 50g plain flour
- 1 beaten egg
- 1 white fish fillet
- The juice of 1 small lemon
- 1 tsp parsley
- 1 tsp thyme
- 1 tsp mixed herbs
- Salt and pepper to taste

Directions:

1. Preheat the air fryer to 180°C
2. Add salt pepper and parsley to the breadcrumbs and combine well
3. Place the egg in another bowl
4. Place the flour in a separate bowl
5. Place the fish into a food processor and add the lemon juice, salt, pepper thyme and mixed herbs
6. Blitz to create a crumb-like consistency
7. Roll your fish in the flour, then the egg and then the breadcrumbs
8. Cook at 180°C for 8 minutes

Beer Battered Fish Tacos

Servings: 2 | Cooking Time:xx

Ingredients:
- 300g cod fillets
- 2 eggs
- 1 can of Mexican beer
- 300g cornstarch
- 300g flour
- 2 soft corn tortillas
- ½ tsp chilli powder
- 1 tbsp cumin
- Salt and pepper to taste

Directions:
1. Whisk together the eggs and beer
2. In a separate bowl whisk together cornstarch, chilli powder, flour, cumin and salt and pepper
3. Coat the fish in the egg mixture then coat in flour mixture
4. Spray the air fryer with non stick spray and add the fish
5. Set your fryer to 170ºC and cook for 15 minutes
6. Place the fish in a corn tortilla

Mahi Fish Tacos

Servings: 4 | Cooking Time:xx

Ingredients:
- 400g fresh mahi
- 8 small corn tortillas
- 2 tsp cajun seasoning
- 5 tbsp sour cream
- 2 tbsp mayonnaise
- 2 tbsp scotch bonnet pepper sauce (use 1 tbsp if you don't like your food too spicy)
- 1 tbsp sriracha sauce
- 2 tbsp lime juice
- Salt and pepper to taste
- 1 tbsp vegetable oil

Directions:
1. Clean the mahi. Cut into half inch slices and season with salt
2. Mix quarter parts cayenne pepper and black pepper with cajun seasoning. Sprinkle onto fish
3. Brush pepper sauce on both sides of the fish
4. Set the air fryer to 180ºC and cook for about 10 minutes or until golden brown
5. Whilst the fish cooks make the chipotle lime cream. Mix the mayo, sour cream, lime juice sriracha and cayenne pepper
6. Assemble tacos and enjoy

Shrimp Wrapped With Bacon

Servings: 2 | Cooking Time:xx

Ingredients:

- 16 shrimp
- 16 slices of bacon
- 2 tbsp ranch dressing to serve

Directions:

1. Preheat the air fryer to 200ºC
2. Wrap the shrimps in the bacon
3. Refrigerate for 30 minutes
4. Cook the shrimp for about 5 minutes turn them over and cook for a further 2 minutes
5. Serve with the ranch dressing on the side

Peppery Lemon Shrimp

Servings: 2 | Cooking Time:xx

Ingredients:

- 300g uncooked shrimp
- 1 tbsp olive oil
- 1 the juice of 1 lemon
- 0.25 tsp garlic powder
- 1 sliced lemon
- 1 tsp pepper
- 0.25 tsp paprika

Directions:

1. Heat the fryer to 200ºC
2. Take a medium sized mixing bowl and combine the lemon juice, pepper, garlic powder, paprika and the olive oil together
3. Add the shrimp to the bowl and make sure they're well coated
4. Arrange the shrimp into the basket of the fryer
5. Cook for between 6-8 minutes, until firm and pink

Furikake Salmon

Servings: 2 | Cooking Time:xx

Ingredients:

- 1 salmon fillet
- 2 tbsp furikake
- 150ml mayonnaise
- 1 tbsp shoe
- Salt and pepper for seasoning

Directions:

1. Preheat the air fryer to 230ºC
2. Take a small bowl and combine the mayonnaise and shoyu
3. Add salt and pepper to the salmon on both sides
4. Place in the air fryer with the skin facing downwards
5. Brush a layer of the mayonnaise mixture on top of the salmon
6. Sprinkle the furikake on top
7. Cook for 10 minutes

Lobster Tails

Servings: 2 | Cooking Time:xx

Ingredients:

- 4 lobster tails
- 2 tbsp melted butter
- ½ tsp salt
- 1 tsp pepper

Directions:

1. Cut the lobster tails through the tail section and pull back the shell
2. Brush with the melted butter and sprinkle with salt and pepper
3. Heat the air fryer to 200ºC and cook for 4 minutes
4. Brush with melted butter and cook for a further 2 minutes

Cod In Parma Ham

Servings: 2 | Cooking Time:xx

Ingredients:

- 2 x 175–190-g/6–7-oz. cod fillets, skin removed
- 6 slices Parma ham or prosciutto
- 16 cherry tomatoes
- 60 g/2 oz. rocket/arugula
- DRESSING
- 1 tablespoon olive oil
- 1½ teaspoons balsamic vinegar
- garlic salt, to taste
- freshly ground black pepper, to taste

Directions:

1. Preheat the air-fryer to 180ºC/350ºF.
2. Wrap each piece of cod snugly in 3 ham slices. Add the ham-wrapped cod fillets and the tomatoes to the preheated air-fryer and air-fry for 6 minutes, turning the cod halfway through cooking. Check the internal temperature of the fish has reached at least 60ºC/140ºF using a meat thermometer – if not, cook for another minute.
3. Meanwhile, make the dressing by combining all the ingredients in a jar and shaking well.
4. Serve the cod and tomatoes on a bed of rocket/arugula with the dressing poured over.

Vegetarian & Vegan
Recipes

Saganaki

Servings: 2 | Cooking Time:xx

Ingredients:
- 200 g/7 oz. kefalotyri or manouri cheese, sliced into wedges 1 cm/½ in. thick
- 2 tablespoons plain/all-purpose flour
- olive oil, for drizzling

Directions:
1. Preheat the air-fryer to 200°C/400°F.
2. Dip each wedge of cheese in the flour, then tap off any excess. Drizzle olive oil onto both sides of the cheese slices
3. Add the cheese to the preheated air-fryer and air-fry for 3 minutes. Remove from the air-fryer and serve.

Bbq Soy Curls

Servings: 2 | Cooking Time:xx

Ingredients:
- 250ml warm water
- 1 tsp vegetable bouillon
- 200g soy curls
- 40g BBQ sauce
- 1 tsp oil

Directions:
1. Soak the soy curls in water and bouillon for 10 minutes
2. Place the soy curls in another bowl and shred
3. Heat the air fryer to 200°C
4. Cook for 3 minutes
5. Remove from the air fryer and coat in bbq sauce
6. Return to the air fryer and cook for 5 minutes shaking halfway through

Spinach And Feta Croissants

Servings:4 | Cooking Time:10 Minutes

Ingredients:

- 4 pre-made croissants
- 100 g / 7 oz feta cheese, crumbled
- 1 tsp dried chives
- 1 tsp garlic powder
- 50 g / 3.5 oz fresh spinach, chopped

Directions:

1. Preheat the air fryer to 180 °C / 350 °F. Remove the mesh basket from the air fryer machine and line with parchment paper.
2. Cut the croissants in half and lay each half out on the lined mesh basket.
3. In a bowl, combine the crumbled feta cheese, dried chives, garlic powder, and chopped spinach until they form a consistent mixture.
4. Spoon some of the mixture one half of the four croissants and cover with the second half of the croissants to seal in the filling.
5. Carefully slide the croissants in the mesh basket into the air fryer machine, close the lid, and cook for 10 minutes until the pastry is crispy and the feta cheese has melted.

Stuffed Peppers

Servings: 6 | Cooking Time:xx

Ingredients:

- 250g diced potatoes
- 100g peas
- 1 small onion, diced
- 1 carrot, diced
- 1 bread roll, diced
- 2 garlic cloves, minced
- 2 tsp mixed herbs
- 6 bell peppers
- 100g grated cheese

Directions:

1. Preheat air fryer to 180°C
2. Combine all the ingredients together apart from the peppers
3. Stuff the peppers with the mix
4. Place in the air fryer and cook for about 20 minutes

Lentil Burgers

Servings: 4 | Cooking Time:xx

Ingredients:

- 100g black buluga lentils
- 1 carrot, grated
- 1 diced onion
- 100g white cabbage
- 300g oats
- 1 tbsp garlic puree
- 1 tsp cumin
- Salt and pepper

Directions:

1. Blend the oats until they resemble flour
2. Put the lentils in a pan with water and cook for 45 minutes
3. Steam your vegetables for 5 minutes
4. Add all the ingredients into a bowl and mix well to combine
5. Form into burgers place in the air fryer and cook at 180ºC for 30 minutes

Falafel Burgers

Servings: 2 | Cooking Time:xx

Ingredients:

- 1 large can of chickpeas
- 1 onion
- 1 lemon
- 140g oats
- 28g grated cheese
- 28g feta cheese
- Salt and pepper to taste
- 3 tbsp Greek yogurt
- 4 tbsp soft cheese
- 1 tbsp garlic puree
- 1 tbsp coriander
- 1 tbsp oregano
- 1 tbsp parsley

Directions:

1. Place the chickpeas, onion, lemon rind, garlic and seasonings and blend until coarse
2. Add the mix to a bowl and stir in half the soft cheese, cheese and feta
3. Form in to burger shape and coat in the oats
4. Place in the air fryer and cook at 180ºC for 8 minutes
5. To make the sauce mix the remaining soft cheese, greek yogurt and lemon juice in a bowl

Camembert & Soldiers

Servings: 2 | Cooking Time:xx

Ingredients:

- 1 piece of Camembert
- 2 slices sandwich bread
- 1 tbsp mustard

Directions:

1. Preheat the air fryer to 180ºC
2. Place the camembert in a sturdy container, cook in the air fryer for 15 minutes
3. Toast the bread and cut into soldiers
4. Serve with the mustard by the side

Roasted Vegetable Pasta

Servings:4 | Cooking Time:15 Minutes

Ingredients:

- 400 g / 14 oz penne pasta
- 1 courgette, sliced
- 1 red pepper, deseeded and sliced
- 100 g / 3.5 oz mushroom, sliced
- 2 tbsp olive oil
- 1 tsp Italian seasoning
- 200 g cherry tomatoes, halved
- 2 tbsp fresh basil, chopped
- ½ tsp black pepper

Directions:

1. Cook the pasta according to the packet instructions.
2. Preheat the air fryer to 190 °C / 370 °F and line the air fryer with parchment paper or grease it with olive oil.
3. In a bowl, place the courgette, pepper, and mushroom, and toss in 2 tbsp olive oil
4. Place the vegetables in the air fryer and cook for 15 minutes.
5. Once the vegetables have softened, mix with the penne pasta, chopped cherry tomatoes, and fresh basil.
6. Serve while hot with a sprinkle of black pepper in each dish.

Roasted Cauliflower

Servings: 2 | Cooking Time:xx

Ingredients:

- 3 cloves garlic
- 1 tbsp peanut oil
- ½ tsp salt
- ½ tsp paprika
- 400g cauliflower florets

Directions:

1. Preheat air fryer to 200ºC
2. Crush the garlic, place all ingredients in a bowl and mix well
3. Place in the air fryer and cook for about 15 minutes, shaking every 5 minutes

Spicy Spanish Potatoes

Servings: 2 | Cooking Time:xx

Ingredients:

- 4 large potatoes
- 1 tbsp olive oil
- 2 tsp paprika
- 2 tsp dried garlic
- 1 tsp barbacoa seasoning
- Salt and pepper

Directions:

1. Chop the potatoes into wedges
2. Place them in a bowl with olive oil and seasoning, mix well
3. Add to the air fryer and cook at 160ºC for 20 minutes
4. Shake, increase heat to 200ºC and cook for another 3 minutes

Buffalo Cauliflower Bites

Servings: 4 | Cooking Time:xx

Ingredients:

- 3 tbsp ketchup
- 2 tbsp hot sauce
- 1 large egg white
- 200g panko bread crumbs
- 400g cauliflower
- ¼ tsp black pepper
- Cooking spray
- 40g sour cream
- 40g blue cheese
- 1 garlic clove, grated
- 1 tsp red wine vinegar

Directions:

1. Whisk together ketchup, hot sauce and egg white
2. Place the breadcrumbs in another bowl
3. Dip the cauliflower in the sauce then in the breadcrumbs
4. Coat with cooking spray
5. Place in the air fryer and cook at 160ºC for about 20 minutes until crispy
6. Mix remaining ingredients together and serve as a dip

Rainbow Vegetables

Servings: 4 | Cooking Time:xx

Ingredients:
- 1 red pepper, cut into slices
- 1 squash sliced
- 1 courgette sliced
- 1 tbsp olive oil
- 150g sliced mushrooms
- 1 onion sliced
- Salt and pepper to taste

Directions:
1. Preheat air fryer to 180ºC
2. Place all ingredients in a bowl and mix well
3. Place in the air fryer and cook for about 20 minutes turning halfway

Mushroom Pasta

Servings: 4 | Cooking Time:xx

Ingredients:
- 250g sliced mushrooms
- 1 chopped onion
- 2 tsp minced garlic
- 1 tsp salt
- ½ tsp red pepper flakes
- 75g cup cream
- 70g mascarpone
- 1 tsp dried thyme
- 1 tsp ground black pepper
- ½ cup grated parmesan

Directions:
1. Place all the ingredients in a bowl and mix well
2. Heat the air fryer to 175ºC
3. Grease a 7x3 inch pan and pour in the mixture
4. Place in the air fryer and cook for 15 minutes stirring halfway through
5. Pour over cooked pasta and sprinkle with parmesan

Roast Vegetables

Servings: 4 | Cooking Time:xx

Ingredients:

- 100g diced courgette
- 100g diced squash
- 100g diced mushrooms
- 100g diced cauliflower
- 100g diced asparagus
- 100g diced pepper
- 2 tsp oil
- ½ tsp salt
- ¼ tsp pepper
- ¼ tsp seasoning

Directions:

1. Preheat air fryer to 180ºC
2. Mix all ingredients together
3. Add to air fryer and cook for 10 minutes stirring halfway

Roast Cauliflower & Broccoli

Servings: 6 | Cooking Time:xx

Ingredients:

- 300g broccoli
- 300g cauliflower
- 2 tbsp oil
- ½ tsp garlic powder
- ¼ tsp salt
- ¼ tsp paprika
- ⅛ tsp pepper

Directions:

1. Preheat air fryer to 200ºC
2. Place broccoli and cauliflower in a bowl and microwave for 3 minutes
3. Add remaining ingredients and mix well
4. Add to the air fryer and cook for about 12 mins

Ravioli Air Fryer Style

Servings: 4 | Cooking Time:xx

Ingredients:

- Half a pack of frozen ravioli
- 200g Italian breadcrumbs
- 200ml buttermilk
- 5 tbsp marinara sauce
- 1 tbsp olive oil

Directions:

1. Preheat the air fryer to 220ºC
2. Place the buttermilk in a bowl
3. Add the breadcrumbs to another bowl
4. Take each piece of ravioli and dip it first into the buttermilk and then into the breadcrumbs, coating evenly
5. Add the ravioli to the air fryer and cook for 7 minutes, adding a small amount of oil at the halfway point
6. Serve with the marinara sauce on the side

Artichoke Pasta

Servings: 2 | Cooking Time:xx

Ingredients:

- 100g pasta
- 50g basil leaves
- 6 artichoke hearts
- 2 tbsp pumpkin seeds
- 2 tbsp lemon juice
- 1 clove garlic
- ½ tsp white miso paste
- 1 can chickpeas
- 1 tsp olive oil

Directions:

1. Place the chickpeas in the air fryer and cook at 200ºC for 12 minutes
2. Cook the pasta according to packet instructions
3. Add the remaining ingredients to a food processor and blend
4. Add the pasta to a bowl and spoon over the pesto mix
5. Serve and top with roasted chickpeas

Veggie Lasagne

Servings: 1 | Cooking Time:xx

Ingredients:

- 2 lasagne sheets
- Pinch of salt
- 100g pasta sauce
- 50g ricotta
- 60g chopped basil
- 40g chopped spinach
- 3 tbsp grated courgette

Directions:

1. Break the lasagne sheets in half, bring a pan of water to boil
2. Cook the lasagne sheets for about 8 minutes, drain and pat dry
3. Add 2 tbsp of pasta sauce to a mini loaf tin
4. Add a lasagne sheet, top with ricotta, basil and spinach, then add courgette
5. Place another lasagne sheet on top
6. Add a couple of tbsp pasta sauce, basil, spinach and courgette
7. Add the last lasagne sheet, top with pasta sauce and ricotta
8. Cover with foil and place in the air fryer
9. Cook at 180ºC for 10 mins, remove foil and cook for another 3 minutes

Air Fryer Cheese Sandwich

Servings:2 | Cooking Time:10 Minutes

Ingredients:

- 4 slices white or wholemeal bread
- 2 tbsp butter
- 50 g / 3.5 oz cheddar cheese, grated

Directions:

1. Preheat the air fryer to 180 °C / 350 °F and line the bottom of the basket with parchment paper.
2. Lay the slices of bread out on a clean surface and butter one side of each. Evenly sprinkle the cheese on two of the slices and cover with the final two slices.
3. Transfer the sandwiches to the air fryer, close the lid, and cook for 5 minutes until the bread is crispy and golden, and the cheese is melted.

Broccoli Cheese

Servings: 2 | Cooking Time:xx

Ingredients:

- 250g broccoli
- Cooking spray
- 10 tbsp evaporated milk
- 300g Mexican cheese
- 4 tsp Amarillo paste
- 6 saltine crackers

Directions:

1. Heat the air fryer to 190ºC
2. Place the broccoli in the air fryer spray with cooking oil and cook for about 6 minutes
3. Place the remaining ingredients in a blender and process until smooth
4. Place in a bowl and microwave for 30 seconds
5. Pour over the broccoli and serve

Side Dishes Recipes

Air Fryer Eggy Bread

Servings:2 | Cooking Time:5-7 Minutes

Ingredients:

- 4 slices white bread
- 4 eggs, beaten
- 1 tsp black pepper
- 1 tsp dried chives

Directions:

1. Preheat your air fryer to 150 °C / 300 °F and line the bottom of the basket with parchment paper.
2. Whisk the eggs in a large mixing bowl and soak each slice of bread until fully coated.
3. Transfer the eggy bread to the preheated air fryer and cook for 5-7 minutes until the eggs are set and the bread is crispy.
4. Serve hot with a sprinkle of black pepper and chives on top.

Carrot & Parmesan Chips

Servings: 2 | Cooking Time:xx

Ingredients:

- 180g carrots
- 1 tbsp olive oil
- 2 tbsp grated parmesan
- 1 crushed garlic clove
- Salt and pepper for seasoning

Directions:

1. Take a mixing bowl and add the olive oil and garlic, combining well
2. Remove the tops of the carrots and cut into halves, and then another half
3. Add the carrots to the bowl and toss well
4. Add the parmesan and coat the carrots well
5. Add the carrots to the air fryer and cook for 20 minutes at 220°C, shaking halfway through

Bbq Beetroot Crisps

Servings:4 | Cooking Time:5 Minutes

Ingredients:

- 400 g / 14 oz beetroot, sliced
- 2 tbsp olive oil
- 1 tbsp BBQ seasoning
- ½ tsp black pepper

Directions:

1. Preheat the air fryer to 180 °C / 350 °F and line the bottom of the basket with parchment paper.
2. Place the beetroot slices in a large bowl. Add the olive oil, BBQ seasoning, and black pepper, and toss to coat the beetroot slices on both sides.
3. Place the beetroot slices in the air fryer and cook for 5 minutes until hot and crispy.

Honey Roasted Parsnips

Servings: 4 | Cooking Time:xx

Ingredients:

- 350 g/12 oz. parsnips
- 1 tablespoon plain/all-purpose flour (gluten-free if you wish)
- 1½ tablespoons runny honey
- 2 tablespoons olive oil
- salt

Directions:

1. Top and tail the parsnips, then slice lengthways, about 2 cm/¾ in. wide. Place in a saucepan with water to cover and a good pinch of salt. Bring to the boil, then boil for 5 minutes.
2. Remove and drain well, allowing any excess water to evaporate. Dust the parsnips with flour. Mix together the honey and oil in a small bowl, then toss in the parsnips to coat well in the honey and oil.
3. Preheat the air-fryer to 180ºC/350ºF.
4. Add the parsnips to the preheated air-fryer and air-fry for 14–16 minutes, depending on how dark you like the outsides (the longer you cook them, the sweeter they get).

Tex Mex Hash Browns

Servings: 4 | Cooking Time:xx

Ingredients:

- 500g potatoes cut into cubes
- 1 tbsp olive oil
- 1 red pepper
- 1 onion
- 1 jalapeño pepper
- ½ tsp taco seasoning
- ½ tsp cumin
- Salt and pepper to taste

Directions:

1. Soak the potatoes in water for 20 minutes
2. Heat the air fryer to 160ºC
3. Drain the potatoes and coat with olive oil
4. Add to the air fryer and cook for 18 minutes
5. Mix the remaining ingredients in a bowl, add the potatoes and mix well
6. Place the mix into the air fryer cook for 6 minutes, shake and cook for a further 5 minutes

Onion Rings

Servings: 4 | Cooking Time:xx

Ingredients:

- 200g flour
- 75g cornstarch
- 2 tsp baking powder
- 1 tsp salt
- 2 pinches of paprika
- 1 large onion, cut into rings
- 1 egg
- 1 cup milk
- 200g breadcrumbs
- 2 pinches garlic powder

Directions:

1. Stir flour, salt, starch and baking powder together in a bowl
2. Dip onion rings into the flour mix to coat
3. Whisk the egg and milk into the flour mix, dip in the onion rings
4. Dip the onion rings into the bread crumbs
5. Heat the air fryer to 200ºC
6. Place the onion rings in the air fryer and cook for 2-3 minutes until golden brown
7. Sprinkle with paprika and garlic powder to serve

Stuffing Filled Pumpkin

Servings: 2 | Cooking Time:xx

Ingredients:

- 1/2 small pumpkin
- 1 diced parsnip
- 1 sweet potato, diced
- 1 diced onion
- 2 tsp dried mixed herbs
- 50g peas
- 1 carrot, diced
- 1 egg
- 2 minced garlic cloves

Directions:

1. Remove the seeds from the pumpkin
2. Combine all the other ingredients in a bowl
3. Stuff the pumpkin
4. Preheat the air fryer to 175ºC
5. Place the pumpkin in the air fryer and cook for about 30 minutes

Orange Sesame Cauliflower

Servings: 4 | Cooking Time:xx

Ingredients:

- 100ml water
- 30g cornstarch
- 50g flour
- 1/2 tsp salt
- ½ tsp pepper
- 2 tbsp tomato ketchup
- 2 tbsp brown sugar
- 1 sliced onion

Directions:

1. Mix together flour, cornstarch, water, salt and pepper until smooth
2. Coat the cauliflower and chill for 30 minutes
3. Place in the air fryer and cook for 22 minutes at 170ºC
4. Meanwhile combine remaining ingredients in a saucepan, gently simmer until thickened.
5. Mix cauliflower with sauce and top with toasted sesame seeds to serve

Stuffed Jacket Potatoes

Servings: 4 | Cooking Time:xx

Ingredients:

- 2 large russet potatoes
- 2 tsp olive oil
- 100ml yoghurt
- 100ml milk
- ¼ tsp pepper
- 50g chopped spinach
- 2 tbsp nutritional yeast
- ½ tsp salt

Directions:

1. Preheat the air fryer to 190ºC
2. Rub the potatoes with oil
3. Place the potatoes in the air fryer and cook for 30 minutes, turn and cook for a further 30 minutes
4. Cut each potato in half and scoop out the middles, mash with yoghurt, milk and yeast. Stir in the spinach and season with salt and pepper
5. Add the mix back into the potato skins and place in the air fryer, cook at 160ºC for about 5 mins

Spicy Green Beans

Servings: 4 | Cooking Time:xx

Ingredients:

- 300g green beans
- 1 tbsp sesame oil
- 1 tsp soy
- 1 tsp rice wine vinegar
- 1 clove garlic, minced
- 1 tsp red pepper flakes

Directions:

1. Preheat air fryer to 200ºC
2. Place green beans in a bowl
3. Mix together remaining ingredients, add green beans and fully coat
4. Place in the air fryer and cook for 12 minutes

Cauliflower With Hot Sauce And Blue Cheese Sauce

Servings:2 | Cooking Time:15 Minutes

Ingredients:

- For the cauliflower:
- 1 cauliflower, broken into florets
- 4 tbsp hot sauce
- 2 tbsp olive oil
- 1 tsp garlic powder
- ½ tsp salt
- ½ tsp black pepper
- 1 tbsp plain flour
- 1 tbsp corn starch
- For the blue cheese sauce:
- 50 g / 1.8 oz blue cheese, crumbled
- 2 tbsp sour cream
- 2 tbsp mayonnaise
- ½ tsp salt
- ½ tsp black pepper

Directions:

1. Preheat the air fryer to 180 °C / 350 °F and line the bottom of the basket with parchment paper.
2. In a bowl, combine the hot sauce, olive oil, garlic powder, salt, and black pepper until it forms a consistent mixture. Add the cauliflower to the bowl and coat in the sauce.
3. Stir in the plain flour and corn starch until well combined.
4. Transfer the cauliflower to the lined basket in the air fryer, close the lid, and cook for 12-15 minutes until the cauliflower has softened and is golden in colour.
5. Meanwhile, make the blue cheese sauce by combining all of the ingredients. When the cauliflower is ready, remove it from the air fryer and serve with the blue cheese sauce on the side.

Yorkshire Puddings

Servings: 2 | Cooking Time:xx

Ingredients:

- 1 tablespoon olive oil
- 70 g/½ cup plus ½ tablespoon plain/all-purpose flour (gluten-free if you wish)
- 100 ml/7 tablespoons milk
- 2 eggs
- salt and freshly ground black pepper

Directions:

1. You will need 4 ramekins. Preheat the air-fryer to 200°C/400°F.
2. Using a pastry brush, oil the base and sides of each ramekin, dividing the oil equally between the ramekins. Place the greased ramekins in the preheated air-fryer and heat for 5 minutes.
3. Meanwhile, in a food processor or using a whisk, combine the flour, milk, eggs and seasoning until you have a batter that is frothy on top. Divide the batter equally between the preheated ramekins. Return the ramekins to the air-fryer and air-fry for 20 minutes without opening the drawer. Remove the Yorkshire puddings from the ramekins and serve immediately.

Alternative Stuffed Potatoes

Servings: 4 | Cooking Time:xx

Ingredients:

- 4 baking potatoes, peeled and halved
- 1 tbsp olive oil
- 150g grated cheese
- ½ onion, diced
- 2 slices bacon

Directions:

1. Preheat air fryer to 175°C
2. Brush the potatoes with oil and cook in the air fryer for 10 minutes
3. Coat again with oil and cook for a further 10 minutes
4. Cut the potatoes in half spoon the insides into a bowl and mix in the cheese
5. Place the bacon and onion in a pan and cook until browned, mix in with the potato
6. Stuff the skins with the mix and return to the air fryer, cook for about 6 minutes

Corn On The Cob

Servings: 4 | Cooking Time:xx

Ingredients:

- 75g mayo
- 2 tsp grated cheese
- 1 tsp lime juice
- ¼ tsp chilli powder
- 2 ears of corn, cut into 4

Directions:

1. Heat the air fryer to 200ºC
2. Mix the mayo, cheese lime juice and chilli powder in a bowl
3. Cover the corn in the mayo mix
4. Place in the air fryer and cook for 8 minutes

Ricotta Stuffed Aubergine

Servings: 2 | Cooking Time:xx

Ingredients:

- 1 aubergine
- 150g ricotta cheese
- 75g Parmesan cheese, plus an extra 75g for the breading
- 1 tsp garlic powder
- 3 tbsp parsley
- 1 egg, plus an extra 2 eggs for the breading
- 300g pork rind crumbs
- 2 tsp Italian seasoning

Directions:

1. Cut the aubergine into rounds, about 1/2" in thickness
2. Line a baking sheet with parchment and arrange the rounds on top, sprinkling with salt
3. Place another sheet of parchment on top and place something heavy on top to get rid of excess water
4. Leave for 30 minutes
5. Take a bowl and combine the egg, ricotta, 75g Parmesan and parsley, until smooth
6. Remove the parchment from the aubergine and wipe off the salt
7. Take a tablespoon of the ricotta mixture and place on top of each round of aubergine, spreading with a knife
8. Place in the freezer for a while to set
9. Take a bowl and add the two eggs, the pork rinds, parmesan and seasonings, and combine
10. Remove the aubergine from the freezer and coat each one in the mixture completely
11. Place back in the freezer for 45 minutes
12. Cook in the air fryer for 8 minutes at 250ºC

Ranch-style Potatoes

Servings: 2 | Cooking Time:xx

Ingredients:

- 300g baby potatoes, washed
- 1 tbsp olive oil
- 3 tbsp dry ranch seasoning

Directions:

1. Preheat the air fryer to 220°C
2. Cut the potatoes in half
3. Take a mixing bowl and combine the olive oil with the ranch seasoning
4. Add the potatoes to the bowl and toss to coat
5. Cook for 15 minutes, shaking halfway through

Roasted Okra

Servings: 1 | Cooking Time:xx

Ingredients:

- 300g Okra, ends trimmed and pods sliced
- 1 tsp olive oil
- ¼ tsp salt
- ⅛ tsp pepper

Directions:

1. Preheat the air fryer to 175°C
2. Combine all ingredients in a bowl and stir gently
3. Place in the air fryer and cook for 5 minutes, shake and cook for another 5 minutes

Super Easy Fries

Servings: 2 | Cooking Time:xx

Ingredients:

- 500g potatoes cut into ½ inch sticks
- 1 tsp olive oil
- ¼ tsp salt
- ¼ tsp pepper

Directions:

1. Place the potatoes in a bowl cover with water and allow to soak for 30 minutes
2. Spread the butter onto one side of the bread slices
3. Pat dry with paper, drizzle with oil and toss to coat
4. Place in the air fryer and cook at 200°C for about 15 minutes, keep tossing through cooking time
5. Sprinkle with salt and pepper

Potato Wedges

Servings: 4 | Cooking Time:xx

Ingredients:

- 2 potatoes, cut into wedges
- 1 ½ tbsp olive oil
- ½ tsp paprika
- ⅛ tsp ground black pepper
- ½ tsp parsley flakes
- ½ tsp chilli powder
- ½ tsp sea salt

Directions:

1. Preheat the air fryer to 200ºC
2. Add all ingredients to a bowl and combine well
3. Place the wedges into the air fryer and cook for 10 minutes
4. Turn and cook for a further 8 minutes until golden brown

Mediterranean Vegetables

Servings: 1–2 | Cooking Time:xx

Ingredients:

- 1 courgette/zucchini, thickly sliced
- 1 (bell) pepper, deseeded and chopped into large chunks
- 1 red onion, sliced into wedges
- 12 cherry tomatoes
- 1 tablespoon olive oil
- ½ teaspoon salt
- ½ teaspoon freshly ground black pepper
- 2 rosemary twigs
- mozzarella, fresh pesto (see page 80) and basil leaves, to serve

Directions:

1. Preheat the air-fryer to 180ºC/350ºF.
2. Toss the prepared vegetables in the oil and seasoning. Add the vegetables and the rosemary to the preheated air-fryer and air-fry for 12–14 minutes, depending on how 'chargrilled' you like them.
3. Remove and serve topped with fresh mozzarella and pesto and scattered with basil leaves.

Desserts Recipes

Oat-covered Banana Fritters

Servings: 4 | Cooking Time:xx

Ingredients:
- 3 tablespoons plain/all-purpose flour (gluten-free if you wish)
- 1 egg, beaten
- 90 g/3 oz. oatcakes (gluten-free if you wish) or oat-based cookies, crushed to a crumb consistency
- 1½ teaspoons ground cinnamon
- 1 tablespoon unrefined sugar
- 4 bananas, peeled

Directions:
1. Preheat the air-fryer to 180ºC/350ºF.
2. Set up three bowls – one with flour, one with beaten egg and the other with the oatcake crumb, cinnamon and sugar mixed together. Coat the bananas in flour, then in egg, then in the crumb mixture.
3. Add the bananas to the preheated air-fryer and air-fry for 10 minutes. Serve warm.

Peach Pies

Servings: 8 | Cooking Time:xx

Ingredients:
- 2 peaches, peeled and chopped
- 1 tbsp lemon juice
- 3 tbsp sugar
- 1 tsp vanilla extract
- ¼ tsp salt
- 1 tsp cornstarch
- 1 pack ready made pastry
- Cooking spray

Directions:
1. Mix together peaches, lemon juice, sugar and vanilla in a bowl. Stand for 15 minutes
2. Drain the peaches keeping 1 tbsp of the liquid, mix cornstarch into the peaches
3. Cut the pastry into 8 circles, fill with the peach mix
4. Brush the edges of the pastry with water and fold over to form half moons, crimp the edges to seal
5. Coat with cooking spray
6. Add to the air fryer and cook at 170ºC for 12 minutes until golden brown

Pecan & Molasses Flapjack

Servings:9 | Cooking Time:xx

Ingredients:
- 120 g/½ cup plus 2 teaspoons butter or plant-based spread, plus extra for greasing
- 40 g/2 tablespoons blackstrap molasses
- 60 g/5 tablespoons unrefined sugar
- 50 g/½ cup chopped pecans
- 200 g/1½ cups porridge oats/steelcut oats (not rolled or jumbo)

Directions:
1. Preheat the air-fryer to 180°C/350°F.
2. Grease and line a 15 x 15-cm/6 x 6-in. baking pan.
3. In a large saucepan melt the butter/spread, molasses and sugar. Once melted, stir in the pecans, then the oats. As soon as they are combined, tip the mixture into the prepared baking pan and cover with foil.
4. Place the foil-covered baking pan in the preheated air-fryer and air-fry for 10 minutes. Remove the foil, then cook for a further 2 minutes to brown the top. Leave to cool, then cut into 9 squares.

Chocolate Mug Cake

Servings: 1 | Cooking Time:xx

Ingredients:
- 30g self raising flour
- 5 tbsp sugar
- 1 tbsp cocoa powder
- 3 tbsp milk
- 3 tsp coconut oil

Directions:
1. Mix all the ingredients together in a mug
2. Heat the air fryer to 200°C
3. Place the mug in the air fryer and cook for 10 minutes

Sweet Potato Dessert Fries

Servings: 4 | Cooking Time:xx

Ingredients:
- 2 sweet potatoes, peeled
- ½ tbsp coconut
- 1 tbsp arrowroot
- 2 tsp melted butter
- ½ cup coconut sugar
- 2 tsp cinnamon
- Icing sugar

Directions:
1. Cut the potatoes into ½ inch thick strips, coat in arrowroot and coconut oil
2. Place in the air fryer and cook at 190°C for 18 minutes shaking halfway through
3. Remove from air fryer and place in a bowl, drizzle with melted butter
4. Mix in sugar and cinnamon
5. Sprinkle with icing sugar to serve

Lemon Pies

Servings: 6 | Cooking Time:xx

Ingredients:

- 1 pack of pastry
- 1 egg beaten
- 200g lemon curd
- 225g powdered sugar
- ½ lemon

Directions:

1. Preheat the air fryer to 180°C
2. Cut out 6 circles from the pastry using a cookie cutter
3. Add 1 tbsp of lemon curd to each circle, brush the edges with egg and fold over
4. Press around the edges of the dough with a fork to seal
5. Brush the pies with the egg and cook in the air fryer for 10 minutes
6. Mix the lemon juice with the powdered sugar to make the icing and drizzle on the cooked pies

White Chocolate Pudding

Servings:2 | Cooking Time:15 Minutes

Ingredients:

- 100 g / 3.5 oz white chocolate
- 50 g brown sugar
- 2 tbsp olive oil
- ½ tsp vanilla extract
- 4 egg whites, plus two egg yolks

Directions:

1. Preheat the air fryer to 180 °C / 350 °F and line the mesh basket with parchment paper or grease it with olive oil.
2. Place the white chocolate in a saucepan and place it over low heat until it melts, being careful not to let the chocolate burn.
3. Stir in the brown sugar, olive oil, and vanilla extract.
4. Whisk the egg whites and egg yolks in a bowl until well combined. Fold a third of the eggs into the white chocolate mixture and stir until it forms a smooth and consistent mixture. Repeat twice more with the other two-thirds of the eggs.
5. Pour the white chocolate pudding mixture evenly into two ramekins and place the ramekins in the lined air fryer basket. Cook for 15 minutes until the pudding is hot and set on top.

Grain-free Millionaire's Shortbread

Servings:9 | Cooking Time:xx

Ingredients:

- BASE
- 60 g/5 tablespoons coconut oil
- 1 tablespoon maple syrup
- ½ teaspoon vanilla extract
- 180 g/1¾ cups ground almonds
- a pinch of salt
- MIDDLE
- 185 g/1⅓ cups dried pitted dates (soak in hot water for at least 20 minutes, then drain)
- 2 tablespoons almond butter
- 90 g/scant ½ cup canned coconut milk (the thick part once it has separated is ideal)
- TOPPING
- 125 g/½ cup coconut oil
- 4 tablespoons cacao powder
- 1 tablespoon maple syrup

Directions:

1. Preheat the air-fryer to 180°C/350°F.
2. To make the base, in a small saucepan melt the coconut oil with the maple syrup and vanilla extract. As soon as the coconut oil is melted, stir in the almonds and the salt off the heat. Press this mixture into a 15 x 15-cm/6 x 6-in. baking pan.
3. Add the baking pan to the preheated air-fryer and cook for 4 minutes, until golden brown on top. Remove from the air-fryer and allow to cool.
4. In a food processor, combine the rehydrated drained dates, almond butter and coconut milk. Once the base is cool, pour this mixture over the base and pop into the freezer to set for an hour.
5. After the base has had 45 minutes in the freezer, make the topping by heating the coconut oil in a saucepan until melted, then whisk in the cacao powder and maple syrup off the heat to make a chocolate syrup. Leave this to cool for 15 minutes, then pour over the set middle layer and return to the freezer for 30 minutes. Cut into 9 squares to serve.

Melting Moments

Servings: 9 | Cooking Time:xx

Ingredients:

- 100g butter
- 75g caster sugar
- 150g self raising flour
- 1 egg
- 50g white chocolate
- 3 tbsp desiccated coconut
- 1 tsp vanilla essence

Directions:

1. Preheat the air fryer to 180°C
2. Cream together the butter and sugar, beat in the egg and vanilla
3. Bash the white chocolate into small pieces
4. Add the flour and chocolate and mix well
5. Roll into 9 small balls and cover in coconut
6. Place in the air fryer and cook for 8 minutes and a further 6 minutes at 160°C

Cinnamon Biscuit Bites

Servings: 16 | Cooking Time:xx

Ingredients:
- 200g flour
- 200g wholewheat flour
- 2 tbsp sugar
- 1 tsp baking powder
- ¼ tsp cinnamon
- ¼ tsp salt
- 4 tbsp butter
- 50ml milk
- Cooking spray
- 300g icing sugar
- 3 tbsp water

Directions:
1. Mix together flour, salt, sugar baking powder and cinnamon in a bowl
2. Add butter and mix until well combined
3. Add milk and form a dough, place dough on a floured surface and knead until smooth
4. Cut into 16 equal pieces and form each piece into a ball
5. Place in the air fryer and cook at 180°C for about 12 minutes
6. Mix together icing sugar and water and coat to serve

Chocolate Orange Fondant

Servings: 4 | Cooking Time:xx

Ingredients:
- 2 tbsp self raising flour
- 4 tbsp caster sugar
- 115g dark chocolate
- 115g butter
- 1 medium orange rind and juice
- 2 eggs

Directions:
1. Preheat the air fryer to 180°C and grease 4 ramekins
2. Place the chocolate and butter in a glass dish and melt over a pan of hot water, stir until the texture is creamy
3. Beat the eggs and sugar together until pale and fluffy
4. Add the orange and egg mix to the chocolate and mix
5. Stir in the flour until fully mixed together
6. Put the mix into the ramekins, place in the air fryer and cook for 12 minutes. Leave to stand for 2 minutes before serving

Apple Fritters

Servings: 4 | Cooking Time:xx

Ingredients:

- 225g self raising flour
- 200g greek yogurt
- 2 tsp sugar
- 1 tbsp cinnamon
- 1 apple peeled and chopped
- 225g icing sugar
- 2 tbsp milk

Directions:

1. Mix the flour, yogurt, sugar, cinnamon and apple together. Knead for about 3 -4 minutes
2. Mix the icing sugar and milk together to make the glaze and set aside
3. Line the air fryer with parchment paper and spray with cooking spray
4. Divide the fritter mix into four, flatten each portion and place in the air fryer
5. Cook at 185ºC for about 15 minutes turning halfway
6. Drizzle with glaze to serve

Apple And Cinnamon Puff Pastry Pies

Servings:8 | Cooking Time:20 Minutes

Ingredients:

- 4 tbsp butter
- 4 tbsp white sugar
- 2 tbsp brown sugar
- 1 tsp cinnamon
- 1 tsp nutmeg
- 1 tsp salt
- 4 apples, peeled and diced
- 2 large sheets puff pastry
- 1 egg

Directions:

1. Preheat the air fryer to 180 °C / 350 °F. Remove the mesh basket from the machine and line it with parchment paper.
2. In a bowl, whisk together the butter, white sugar, brown sugar, cinnamon, nutmeg, and salt.
3. Place the apples in a heatproof baking dish and coat them in the butter and sugar mixture. Transfer to the air fryer and cook for 10 minutes.
4. Meanwhile, roll out the pastry on a clean, floured surface. Cut the sheets into 8 equal parts.
5. Once the apples are hot and softened, evenly spread the mixture between the pastry sheets. Fold the sheets over to cover the apple and gently press the edges using a fork or your fingers to seal the mixture in.
6. Beat the egg in a bowl and use a brush to coat the top of each pastry sheet.
7. Carefully transfer the filled pastry sheets to the prepared air fryer basket, close the lid, and cook for 10 minutes until the pastry is golden and crispy.

Birthday Cheesecake

Servings: 8 | Cooking Time:xx

Ingredients:

- 6 Digestive biscuits
- 50g melted butter
- 800g soft cheese
- 500g caster sugar
- 4 tbsp cocoa powder
- 6 eggs
- 2 tbsp honey
- 1 tbsp vanilla

Directions:

1. Flour a spring form tin to prevent sticking
2. Crush the biscuits and then mix with the melted butter, press into the bottom and sides of the tin
3. Mix the caster sugar and soft cheese with an electric mixer. Add 5 eggs, honey and vanilla. Mix well
4. Spoon half the mix into the pan and pat down well. Place in the air fryer and cook at 180ºC for 20 minutes then 160ºC for 15 minutes and then 150ºC for 20 minutes
5. Mix the cocoa and the last egg into the remaining mix. Spoon over the over the bottom layer and place in the fridge. Chill for 11 hours

Mini Egg Buns

Servings: 8 | Cooking Time:xx

Ingredients:

- 100g self raising flour
- 100g caster sugar
- 100g butter
- 2 eggs
- 2 tbsp honey
- 1 tbsp vanilla essence
- 300g soft cheese
- 100g icing sugar
- 2 packets of Mini Eggs

Directions:

1. Cream the butter and sugar together until light and fluffy, beat in the eggs one at a time
2. Add the honey and vanilla essence, fold in the flour a bit at a time
3. Divide the mix into 8 bun cases and place in the air fryer. Cook at 180ºC for about 20 minutes
4. Cream the soft cheese and icing sugar together to make the topping
5. Allow the buns to cool, pipe on the topping mix and add mini eggs

Butter Cake

Servings: 4 | Cooking Time:xx

Ingredients:

- Cooking spray
- 7 tbsp butter
- 25g white sugar
- 2 tbsp white sugar
- 1 egg
- 300g flour
- Pinch salt
- 6 tbsp milk

Directions:

1. Preheat air fryer to 175ºC
2. Spray a small fluted tube pan with cooking spray
3. Beat the butter and all of the sugar together in a bowl until creamy
4. Add the egg and mix until fluffy, add the salt and flour mix well. Add the milk and mix well
5. Put the mix in the pan and cook in the air fryer for 15 minutes

Zebra Cake

Servings: 6 | Cooking Time:xx

Ingredients:

- 115g butter
- 2 eggs
- 100g caster sugar
- 1 tbsp cocoa powder
- 100g self raising flour
- 30ml milk
- 1tsp vanilla

Directions:

1. Preheat air fryer to 160ºC
2. Line a 6 inch baking tin
3. Beat together the butter and sugar until light and fluffy
4. Add eggs one at a time then add the vanilla and milk
5. Add the flour and mix well
6. Divide the mix in half
7. Add cocoa powder to half the mix and mix well
8. Add a scoop of each of the batters at a time until it's all in the tin, place in the air fryer and cook for 30 minutes

Brazilian Pineapple

Servings: 2 | Cooking Time:xx

Ingredients:

- 1 small pineapple, cut into spears
- 100g brown sugar
- 2 tsp cinnamon
- 3 tbsp melted butter

Directions:

1. Mix the brown sugar and cinnamon together in a small bowl
2. Brush the pineapple with melted butter
3. Sprinkle with the sugar and cinnamon
4. Heat the air fryer to 200ºC
5. Cook the pineapple for about 10 minutes

Apple Pie

Servings: 2 | Cooking Time:xx

Ingredients:

- 1 packet of ready made pastry
- 1 apple, chopped
- 2 tsp lemon juice
- 1 tsp cinnamon
- 2 tbsp sugar
- ½ tsp vanilla extract
- 1 tbsp butter
- 1 beaten egg
- 1 tbsp raw sugar

Directions:

1. Preheat the air fryer to 160ºC
2. Line a baking tin with pastry
3. Mix the apple, lemon juice, cinnamon, sugar and vanilla in a bowl
4. Pour the apple mix into the tin with the pastry, top with chunks of butter
5. Cover with a second piece of pastry, place three slits in the top of the pastry
6. Brush the pastry with beaten egg and sprinkle with raw sugar
7. Place in the air fryer and cook for 30 minutes

Chocolate Eclairs

Servings: 9 | Cooking Time:xx

Ingredients:

- 100g plain flour
- 50g butter
- 3 eggs
- 150ml water
- 25g butter
- 1 tsp vanilla extract
- 1 tsp icing sugar
- 150ml whipped cream
- 50g milk chocolate
- 1 tbsp whipped cream

Directions:

1. Preheat the air fryer to 180ºC
2. Add 50g of butter to a pan along with the water and melt over a medium heat
3. Remove from the heat and stir in the flour. Return to the heat until mix form a single ball of dough
4. Allow to cool, once cool beat in the eggs until you have a smooth dough
5. Make into eclair shapes, cook in the air fryer at 180ºC for 10 minutes and then 160ºC for 8 minutes
6. Mix the vanilla, icing sugar and 150ml of whipping cream until nice and thick
7. Once cool fill each eclair with the cream mix
8. Place the chocolate, 1 tbsp whipped cream and 25g of butter in a glass bowl and melt over a pan of boiling water. Top the eclairs

Appendix : Recipes Index

A

Air Fried Maple Chicken Thighs 37
Air Fried Scallops 52
Air Fryer Cheese Sandwich 69
Air Fryer Chicken Thigh Schnitzel 36
Air Fryer Eggy Bread 71
Air Fryer Mussels 51
Air-fried Pickles 21
Alternative Stuffed Potatoes 76
Apple And Cinnamon Puff Pastry Pies 86
Apple Fritters 86
Apple Pie 89
Artichoke Pasta 68
Asparagus & Steak Parcels 46

B

Baba Ganoush 10
Bacon Smokies 24
Bbq Beetroot Crisps 72
Bbq Soy Curls 61
Beef Bulgogi Burgers 43
Beef Kebobs 47
Beef Wellington 45
Beer Battered Fish Tacos 57
Beetroot Crisps 20
Birthday Cheesecake 87
Blanket Breakfast Eggs 16
Blueberry Bread 16
Bocconcini Balls 10
Brazilian Pineapple 89
Breakfast "pop Tarts" 14
Breakfast Doughnuts 16
Breakfast Eggs & Spinach 13
Broccoli Cheese 69
Buffalo Cauliflower Bites 65
Buffalo Chicken Wontons 37
Butter Cake 88
Buttermilk Pork Chops 42

C

Camembert & Soldiers 64
Carrot & Parmesan Chips 71
Cauliflower With Hot Sauce And Blue Cheese Sauce 75
Char Siu Buffalo 42
Chicken And Wheat Stir Fry 39
Chicken Balls, Greek-style 34
Chicken Fajitas 35
Chicken Fried Rice 38
Chicken Jalfrezi 31
Chicken Tikka Masala 32
Chicken Tikka 30
Chocolate Eclairs 90
Chocolate Mug Cake 82
Chocolate Orange Fondant 85
Cinnamon Biscuit Bites 85
Coconut Shrimp 55
Cod In Parma Ham 59
Copycat Fish Fingers 56
Corn Nuts 27
Corn On The Cob 77
Crispy Nacho Prawns 52
Crunchy Chicken Tenders 31
Crunchy Fish 54

E

Easy Cheese & Bacon Toasties 14
European Pancakes 13

F

Falafel Burgers 63
Focaccia Bread 22
French Toast Slices 18
Furikake Salmon 58

G

Garlic Butter Salmon 54
Grain-free Millionaire's Shortbread 84

H

Halloumi Fries 11
Hamburgers 41
Hawaiian Chicken 36

Healthy Bang Bang Chicken 30
Healthy Stuffed Peppers 12
Honey Cajun Chicken Thighs 35
Honey Roasted Parsnips 72
Honey Sriracha Salmon 56

J

Jalapeño Poppers 25
Jamaican Jerk Pork 47

K

Keto Tandoori Chicken 33

L

Lemon Pepper Shrimp 51
Lemon Pies 83
Lentil Burgers 63
Lobster Tails 59

M

Mahi Fish Tacos 57
Meatballs In Tomato Sauce 49
Meatloaf 48
Mediterranean Vegetables 79
Melting Moments 84
Mexican Breakfast Burritos 18
Mini Calzones 23
Mini Egg Buns 87
Monte Cristo Breakfast Sandwich 17
Mushroom Pasta 66
Mustard Pork Tenderloin 44

N

Nashville Chicken 34

O

Oat-covered Banana Fritters 81
Onion Pakoda 28
Onion Rings 73
Orange Chicken 33
Orange Sesame Cauliflower 74

P

Pasta Chips 25
Peach Pies 81
Pecan & Molasses Flapjack 82
Pepperoni Bread 26
Peppers With Aioli Dip 26
Peppery Lemon Shrimp 58
Pitta Pizza 15
Pizza Chicken Nuggets 38
Pork Belly With Crackling 47
Pork Chops With Honey 49
Potato & Chorizo Frittata 12
Potato Wedges 79
Pretzel Bites 24

R

Rainbow Vegetables 66
Ranch-style Potatoes 78
Raspberry Breakfast Pockets 15
Ravioli Air Fryer Style 67
Ricotta Stuffed Aubergine 77
Roast Cauliflower & Broccoli 67
Roast Vegetables 67
Roasted Cauliflower 64
Roasted Okra 78
Roasted Vegetable Pasta 64

S

Saganaki 61
Salmon Patties 52
Salt And Pepper Belly Pork 44
Salt And Vinegar Chips 28
Sausage Gnocchi One Pot 46
Scotch Eggs 22
Shrimp With Yum Yum Sauce 55
Shrimp Wrapped With Bacon 58
Snack Style Falafel 23
Spicy Egg Rolls 20
Spicy Green Beans 75
Spicy Spanish Potatoes 65
Spinach And Feta Croissants 62
Steak Dinner 43
Steak Fajitas 45
Steak Popcorn Bites 41
Store-cupboard Fishcakes 53

Stuffed Jacket Potatoes 74
Stuffed Peppers 62
Stuffing Filled Pumpkin 73
Super Easy Fries 78
Sweet Potato Crisps 27
Sweet Potato Dessert Fries 82
Sweet Potato Fries 17

T

Tandoori Salmon 53
Tasty Pumpkin Seeds 21
Tender Ham Steaks 44
Tex Mex Hash Browns 72
Thai Bites 25
Thai Turkey Burgers 32
Toad In The Hole, Breakfast Style 11
Traditional Pork Chops 48
Turkey Cutlets In Mushroom Sauce 39

V

Veggie Lasagne 68

W

Waffle Fries 21
White Chocolate Pudding 83

Y

Yorkshire Puddings 76
Your Favourite Breakfast Bacon 15

Z

Zebra Cake 88

Printed in Great Britain
by Amazon

30558138R00057